# *Best* Garden Plants *for* New York State

Gardenia
$44  4 feet
x 4 feet
very scented
white

*Maria Cinque • Alison Beck*

LONE PINE

Lone Pine Publishing International

**The Distributor: Lone Pine Publishing**
1808 B Street NW, Suite 140
Auburn, WA, USA  98001
Website: www.lonepinepublishing.com

**Library and Archives Canada Cataloguing in Publication**

Cinque, Maria T.
    Best garden plants for New York State / Maria T. Cinque, Alison Beck.

Includes index.
ISBN-13: 978-9-7682-0033-4

    1. Plants, Ornamental—New York (State). 2. Gardening—New York (State).
I. Beck, Alison, 1971– II. Title.

SB453.2.N7C55 2007              635.9'09747              C2006-905621-8

Front cover photographs by Tim Matheson and Tamara Eder except where noted. *Clockwise from top right:* rose, iris, lilac, daylily, sweet potato vine, daylily, daylily *(Laura Peters)*, dahlia, crabapple, lily *(Erika Flatt)*.

*Photography:* All photos by Tim Matheson, Tamara Eder, Laura Peters and Allison Penko except: AARS 9a, 117, 118a&b, 121a&b; AASelection 12a; Pam Beck 95a&b; Joan de Grey 143b; Therese D'Monte 145b; Don Doucette 98b, 110b; Jen Fafard 140a; Derek Fell 27, 104a, 105, 141a, 145a; Erika Flatt 9b, 89a, 111b, 135b, 144a, 167a; Anne Gordon 146b; Lynne Harrison 101a&b; Richard Hawke-Chicago Botanical Gardens 48a; Saxon Holt 141b, 146a; Jackson & Perkins 116, 122; Duncan Kelbaugh 135a; Debra Knapke 59a; Colin Laroque 66b; Dawn Loewen 72a, 90a; Janet Loughrey 80a, 112a&b; Marilynn McAra 140b, 142b, 143a; Kim O'Leary 11b, 21a&b, 71a, 124b, 134a, 138a; Photos.com 44a, 142a, 147a; Robert Ritchie 45a, 68a, 81a&b, 96a, 151a; Leila Sidi 147b; Vincent Simeone 92a&b; Joy Spurr 123a; Alan Stentz-Missouri Botanical Gardens 115; Peter Thompstone 17a, 56b, 58a; Mark Turner 66a, 80b, 99a, 106a; Valleybrook Gardens 59b; Don Williamson 56a, 127b, 137a&b, 149a; Tim Wood 68b, 75a, 79a, 104b, 113a, 114a.

This book is not intended as a "how-to" guide for eating garden plants. No plant or plant extract should be consumed unless you are certain of its identity and toxicity and of your potential for allergic reactions.

*PC:* P13

# Table of Contents

# Introduction

Starting a garden can be exciting and very rewarding. If you are developing your first garden, it can be a little scary, but that fear can be easily overcome when you think of the beauty you will be creating. If you are afraid of making mistakes, keep in mind that all gardeners make mistakes and that is how we learn. Plus, most mistakes can be undone.

Since there are so many plants for you to choose from, you might find it difficult to decide which ones are suitable for your garden. This book is designed to give beginning gardeners the information they need to start planning and planting gardens of their very own. It includes a wide variety of plants and provides basic descriptions of their characteristics, planting and growing information and tips for use. It will help you get started and put you on your way to producing a beautiful and functional landscape.

New York State encompasses incredible geographical diversity, including a range of habitats: the Appalachian Mountains and plateau; urban centers such as New York City and Albany; lowlands near Lake Champlain; river valleys such as the Hudson River; and the coastal and warmer regions along the Atlantic Ocean, most notably Long Island. Every part of the state provides a unique gardening experience.

In general, New York has a humid continental climate, with strong influences from other climatic regions: maritime influences from the Atlantic, cold and dry influences from the interior, and hot, moist influences from the South and the Gulf of Mexico. For most of the state, the summer growing season is long and warm, and winters are cold enough to ensure a good period of dormancy and plenty of flowers in spring. Rainfall is fairly predictable, but droughts and rainy seasons do occur. The soil, though not without its challenges, supports a variety of healthy plants.

Hardiness zones and frost dates are two terms often used when discussing climate and gardening. Hardiness zones are based on the minimum (lowest) possible winter temperatures. Plants are rated based on the zones in which they grow successfully. Knowing the last-frost date in spring and the first frost date in fall allows us to predict the length of the growing season and gives us an idea of when we can begin planting in spring. The hardiness zones for New York State span from 3 to 7. The lower the zone number, the colder the zone.

Microclimates are small areas that are generally warmer or colder than the surrounding area. Buildings, fences, trees and other large structures can provide extra shelter in winter but may trap heat in summer, thus creating a warmer microclimate. The bottoms of hills are usually colder than the tops but they may not be as windy. Keep these areas in mind when you plan your garden and select your plants; it is possible that you can even grow out-of-zone plants successfully in a warm, sheltered location.

### Getting Started

When planning your garden, start with a quick analysis of the garden as it is now. Plants have different requirements and it is best to put the right plant in the right place rather than to try and change your garden to suit the plants you want. A good place for information on the right plants for your geographic area as well as disease and insect varieties is your local Cornell Cooperative Extension office.

Knowing which parts of your garden receive the most and least amounts of sunlight will help you choose the proper plants and decide where to place them. Light is classified into four basic groups: full sun (direct, unobstructed light all or most of the day); partial shade (direct sun for about half the day and shade for the rest); light shade (shade all or most of the day with some sun filtering through to ground level); and full shade (no direct sunlight). Most plants prefer a certain amount of light, but many can adapt to a range of light levels.

The soil is the foundation of a good garden. Plants need the soil to anchor them to the ground, but most importantly, they receive water, nutrients, organic

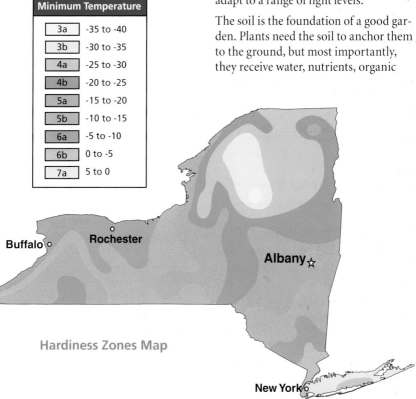

| Average Annual Minimum Temperature | |
| --- | --- |
| 3a | -35 to -40 |
| 3b | -30 to -35 |
| 4a | -25 to -30 |
| 4b | -20 to -25 |
| 5a | -15 to -20 |
| 5b | -10 to -15 |
| 6a | -5 to -10 |
| 6b | 0 to -5 |
| 7a | 5 to 0 |

Buffalo
Rochester
Albany
New York

Hardiness Zones Map

matter and beneficial microorganisms from it. The particle size of the soil influences the amount of air, water and nutrients it can hold. Sand, with the largest particles, has lots of air space and allows water and nutrients to drain quickly. Clay, with the smallest particles, is high in nutrients but has very little air space. Water is therefore slow to penetrate clay and slow to drain from it.

Soil acidity or alkalinity (measured on the pH scale) influences the amount and type of nutrients available to plants. A pH of 7 is neutral; a lower pH is more acidic. Most plants prefer a soil with a pH of 5.5–7.5. Soil-testing kits are available at most garden centers and soil samples can be sent to testing facilities for a more thorough analysis. The results will give you an idea of what plants will do well in your soil and what amendments your soil might need.

Compost is one of the best and most important amendments you can mix into any type of soil. Compost improves the soil by adding organic matter, nutrients and healthy soil microorganisms. It also increases water retention and improves drainage. Compost can be purchased or you can make it in your own backyard. If compost is not available, peat moss is a good alternative.

### Selecting Plants

It's important to purchase healthy plants that are free of insects and diseases. Such plants will establish quickly in your garden and won't introduce problems that may spread to other plants. Plants native to your area are also an option. You should have a good idea of what the plant is supposed to look like—the color and shape of the leaves and the habit of the plant. Inspect the plant for signs of insect damage and diseases.

The majority of plants are container-grown, which is an efficient way for nurseries and greenhouses to grow plants. However, when plants grow in a restricted space for too long, they can become pot bound with their roots densely encircling the inside of the pot. Avoid purchasing plants in this condition; they are often stressed and can take longer to establish. It is often possible to remove pots temporarily to look at the condition of the roots. You can check for soil-borne insects, root rot and girdling or pot-bound roots at the same time. Roots wrapping densely around the inside of a pot must be lightly pruned or teased (slightly and gently pulled) apart before planting.

### Planting Basics

The following tips apply to all plants.

- *Prepare the garden before planting.* If you are starting a new landscape, remove weeds, add any needed amendments and dig or till the soil in preparation for planting. In established beds to which you want to add a single plant

Gently remove container.

Ensure proper planting depth.

Backfill with soil.

you should loosen the soil and work in some compost where you want to plant. The prepared area should be the size of the plant's anticipated mature root system.

• *Settle the soil with water.* Good contact between the roots and the soil is important, but if you press the soil down too firmly, as often happens when you step on the soil, you can compact it, which reduces the movement of water through the soil and leaves fewer air spaces. Instead, pour water in as you fill the hole with soil. The water will settle the soil evenly without allowing it to compact.

• *Unwrap the roots.* It is always best to remove any container before planting to give roots the chance to spread out naturally when planted. In particular, you should remove plastic containers, fiber pots, wire and burlap before planting trees. Fiber pots decompose very slowly, if at all, and they draw moisture away from the plant. Burlap may be synthetic, which won't decompose, and wire can eventually strangle the roots as they mature. The only exceptions to this rule are the peat pots and pellets used to start annuals and vegetables; these decompose and can be planted with the young transplants. Even so, you should slice off some of the sides of these peat pots so that any of the pot that is exposed above ground can be removed to prevent

water from being taken away from the roots.

• *Accommodate the rootball.* If you prepared your planting area ahead of time so it will be big enough for the mature roots, your planting hole will only need to be big enough to accommodate the rootball with the roots spread out slightly.

• *Know the mature size.* Now is the time to consider how big the plants will grow, rather than how big they are at planting time. Large plants should have enough room to mature without interfering with walls, roof overhangs, power lines, walkways and surrounding plants.

• *Plant at the same depth.* Plants generally like to grow at a certain level in relation to the soil and should be planted at the same level they were at in the pot or container before you transplanted them.

• *Identify your plants.* Keep track of what's what in your garden by putting a tag next to each plant when you plant it. A gardening journal is also a great place to list the plants you have and where you planted them. It is very easy for beginning and seasoned gardeners alike to forget exactly what they planted and where they planted it.

• *Water deeply.* It's better to water deeply once every week or two, depending on the plant, than to water a little bit more

Settle backfilled soil with water.

Water the plant well.

Add a layer of mulch.

often. Deep and thorough watering forces roots to grow as they search for water and helps them survive dry spells when water bans may restrict your watering regime. Always check the rootzone before you water, because some soils hold more water for longer periods than other soils. More gardeners overwater than underwater. A general rule on watering when rainfall is lacking is to irrigate new plantings the first year (during the hot months) with 1" of water per week. The second year, they should receive 1" of water every other week and the third year, 1" of water every third week. Mulching helps retain moisture and reduces watering needs. Containers are the watering exception—they can dry out quickly and may even need watering every day.

### Choosing Plants

When choosing the plants you want, try to aim for a variety of sizes, shapes, textures, features and bloom times. Features like decorative fruit, variegated or colorful leaves and interesting bark provide interest when plants aren't blooming and even in the dormant season. This way you will have a garden that captivates your attention all year long.

### Annuals

Annuals are planted new each year and are only expected to last for a single growing season. Their flowers and decorative foliage provide bright splashes of color and can fill in spaces around immature trees, shrubs and perennials.

Annuals are usually sold in small cell-packs of four or six. The roots quickly fill the space in these small packs, so break up the small rootball before you plant. You can run your thumb up each side to break up the roots.

Many annuals are grown from seed, and you can start the seeds directly in the garden once the soil begins to warm up in the spring.

### Perennials

Perennials can live a long time, ranging from a few years to a lifetime. They usually die back to the ground each fall and send up new shoots in spring, though they can also be evergreen or semi-shrubby. They often have a shorter period of bloom than annuals, but they require less care.

Many perennials benefit from being divided every few years, usually in early spring while plants are still dormant or, in some cases, after flowering or in fall. Dividing keeps them growing and blooming vigorously, and in some cases controls their spread. Dividing involves digging a plant up, removing dead debris, breaking the plant into several pieces using a sharp knife, spade or saw and replanting some or all of the pieces. Share the extra pieces with family, friends and neighbors.

### Trees & Shrubs

Trees and shrubs provide the backbone of the garden. They are often the slowest growing plants, but they usually live the longest. Characterized by leaf type, they

Trees and shrubs provide backbone to the mixed border.

Roses are lovely on their own or in mixed borders.

Lilies bloom throughout the summer.

may be deciduous or evergreen, and needled or broad-leaved.

Trees should have as little disturbed soil as possible at the bottom of the planting hole. Loose dirt settles over time and sinking even an inch can kill some trees. The prepared area for trees and shrubs needs to be at least two to four times bigger than the rootball.

Staking, sometimes recommended for newly planted trees, is only necessary for trees over 5' tall. Stakes support the rootball until it grows enough to support the tree. Stakes should allow the trunk to move with the wind without disturbing the rootball.

Pruning is required more often for shrubs than trees. It helps them maintain an attractive shape and can improve blooming. Older, large shade trees should be pruned for safety.

### Roses

Roses are beautiful shrubs with lovely, often fragrant blooms. Traditionally, most roses bloomed only once in the growing season, but new varieties bloom all, or almost all, summer. Repeat-blooming, or recurrent, roses should be deadheaded to encourage more flower production. The flowers on one-time bloomers should be left in place for the colorful hips that develop.

Generally, roses prefer a fertile, well-prepared planting area. A rule of thumb is to prepare an area 24" across, front to back and side to side, and 24" deep. Add plenty of compost or other fertile organic matter and keep roses well watered during the growing season. Many roses are quite durable and will adapt to poorer conditions. Grafted roses should be planted with the graft 2" below the soil line. When watering, avoid getting water on the foliage to reduce the spread of the disease called blackspot.

### Vines

Vines or climbing plants are useful for screening and shade, especially in a location too small for a tree. They may be woody or herbaceous, and annual or perennial. Vines may physically cling to surfaces, they may have wrapping tendrils or stems or they may need to be tied in place with string.

Sturdy trellises, arbors, porch railings, fences, walls, poles and trees are all possible vine supports. If a support is

Many herbs grow well in pots.

needed, make sure it's in place before you plant, to avoid disturbing the roots later. Choose a support that is suitable for the vine you are growing. It needs to be sturdy enough to hold the plant up and should match the growing habit of the vine.

### Bulbs, Corms & Tubers
These plants have fleshy underground storage organs that allow them to survive extended periods of dormancy. They are often grown for the bright splashes of color their flowers provide. They may be spring, summer or fall flowering. Each has an ideal depth and time of year at which it should be planted.

Hardy bulbs can be left in the ground and will flower every year. Some popular tender plants grown from bulbs, corms or tubers are generally lifted from the garden in late summer or fall as the foliage dies back. They are stored in a cool, frost-free location for winter, to be replanted in spring.

### Herbs
Herbs are plants with medicinal, culinary or other economic purposes. A few common culinary herbs are included in this book. Even if you don't cook with them, the often fragrant foliage adds its aroma to the garden, and the plants can be quite decorative in form, leaf and flower. A conveniently placed container—perhaps near the kitchen door—of your favorite herbs will yield plenty of flavor and fragrance all summer.

Many herbs have pollen-producing flowers that attract butterflies, bees, hummingbirds and predatory insects to your garden. Predatory insects feast on problem insects such as aphids, mealy bugs and whiteflies.

### Foliage Plants
Many plants are grown for their decorative foliage rather than their flowers, which may also be decorative. Many of these plants are included elsewhere in the book, but we have featured a few in this section for the unique touch their foliage adds to the garden. Ornamental grasses, ferns, groundcovers and other foliage plants add a variety of colors, textures and forms.

Ornamental grasses and grass-like plants provide interest even in winter if the withered blades are left standing. Cut these grasses back in early spring and divide them when the clumps begin to die out in the centers.

Ferns provide a lacy foliage accent and combine attractively with broad-leaved perennials and shrubs. They are a common sight in moist and shady gardens, and some ferns will even survive in full sun.

### A Final Comment
The more you discover about the fascinating world of plants, whether it be from books, talking to other gardeners, appreciating the creative designs of others or experimenting with something new in your own garden, the more rewarding your gardening experience will be. This book is intended as a guide to germinate and grow your passion for plants. Have fun!

# Begonia
*Begonia*

Begonias have beautiful flowers, compact habits and decorative foliage. They come in a number of varieties, and there is sure to be a begonia to fulfill your shade-gardening needs.

## Growing

Begonias prefer **light or partial shade,** though some wax begonias tolerate sun if their soil is kept moist. The soil should be **fertile, rich in organic matter** and **well drained** with a **neutral or acidic pH**. Allow the soil to dry out slightly between waterings, particularly for tuberous begonias. Begonias love warm weather, so don't plant them before the safe planting date in spring. If they sit in cold soil, they may become stunted and fail to thrive.

## Tips

All begonias are useful for shaded garden beds and planters. The trailing tuberous varieties can be used in hanging baskets and along rock walls where the flowers will cascade over the edges. Wax begonias have a neat, rounded habit that makes them particularly attractive as edging plants. Rex begonias, with their dramatic foliage, are useful as specimen plants in containers and beds.

## Recommended

*B. Rex Cultorum* **Hybrids** (rex begonias) are grown for their dramatic, colorful foliage.

*B. semperflorens* (wax begonias) have pink, white, red or bicolored flowers and green, bronze, reddish or white-variegated foliage.

---

**Features:** colorful pink, white, red, yellow, orange, bicolored flowers; decorative foliage
**Height:** 6–24"  **Spread:** 6–24"

*B. Rex Cultorum* hybrids 'Escargot' (above)
*B. semperflorens* (below)

*B.* x *tuberhybrida* (tuberous begonias) are generally sold as tubers and are popular for their flowers, which grow in many shades of red, pink, yellow, orange or white.

# Black-Eyed Susan

*Rudbeckia*

R. hirta 'Prairie Sun' (above), R. hirta (below)

ⓑlack-eyed Susan brightens up any spot in the garden, and its tolerance for a wide variety of soils from heavy to sandy makes it a very versatile plant. It can be used in new housing developments where the topsoil is often very thin. It is also drought tolerant.

*Black-eyed Susan makes a long-lasting vase flower.*

## Growing

Black-eyed Susan grows equally well in **full sun** or **partial shade**. The soil should be of **average fertility, humus rich, moist** and **well drained**. This plant tolerates heavy clay soil and hot weather. If it is growing in loose, moist soil, black-eyed Susan may reseed itself. Plants can be purchased, started from seed early indoors or directly sown in the garden around the last-frost date. Deadhead to prolong blooming.

## Tips

Plant black-eyed Susan individually or in groups. Use it in beds and borders, large containers, meadow plantings and wildflower gardens. This plant will bloom well, even in the hottest part of the garden.

## Recommended

*R. hirta* forms a bristly mound of foliage and bears bright yellow, daisy-like flowers with brown centers in summer and fall. A wide variety of cultivars are available, including All-America Selections winners **'Cherokee Sunset'** (2003), **'Prairie Sun'** (2003) and **'Indian Summer'** (1995).

Perennial selections of black-eyed Susan are also available, including *R. nitida* **'Autumn Sun,'** a Long Island Gold Medal Award winner. It is an upright, spreading plant that can grow up to 6' tall and spread to 3'. It bears bright golden yellow flowers with green centers from late summer to fall.

**Also called:** coneflower **Features:** colorful yellow, orange, red, brown, sometimes bicolored flowers with brown or green centers **Height:** 8–36" or more **Spread:** 12–18"

# Blanket Flower

*Gaillardia*

G. *pulchella* 'Arizona Sun' (above)

This native annual, with its richly colored blooms, is sure to turn up the heat in your garden.

## Growing

Blanket flower prefers **full sun**. The soil can be of **poor to average fertility, light, sandy** and **well drained**. The less water this plant receives, the better it will do. It is drought tolerant. Deadhead to encourage more blooms. Seeds should be planted once the soil is warm and should be left uncovered because they require light for germination.

## Tips

Blanket flower has an informal habit that makes it a perfect addition to a casual cottage garden or mixed border. Because it is drought tolerant, it is well suited to exposed, sunny slopes, where it can help retain the soil while more permanent plants grow in.

**Features:** red, orange, yellow, bi- or tricolored flowers all summer; bushy habit
**Height:** 12–18" **Spread:** 12–18"

## Recommended

*G.* **'Arizona Sun'** is a 2005 All-America Selections winner. It is a short-lived perennial that is treated like an annual. It forms a low, dense mound that is covered in bright red blooms with yellow petal tips all summer. Plants grow about 12" tall and spread 12–18".

*G.* **'Sundance Bicolor'** is a 2003 All-America Selections winner that forms a bushy mound of foliage and bears bushy, red or orange, yellow-tipped double flowers. Plants grow 12–18" tall, with an equal spread.

# Celosia
*Celosia*

C. *argentea* Plumosa Group (above)
C. *argentea* Cristata Group (below)

From the mysterious, rippled curls of the crested celosias to the soft, dense heads of the plume celosias, these plants are wonderful additions to the garden. Their bright colors and compact growth are sure to draw the attention of passers by.

## Growing

Celosias prefer a **sheltered** spot in **full sun**. The soil should be **fertile, humus rich, moist** and **well drained**. Don't disturb or damage the roots when transplanting seedlings, because the plants can become stunted. Start plants in peat pots or sow them directly in the garden to reduce the chance of damage.

## Tips

Use celosias in borders, beds and planters. The flowers make interesting additions to cut arrangements, either fresh or dried. A mass planting of plume celosias looks bright and cheerful in the garden. The popular crested varieties work well as accents, though they will certainly draw attention if mass planted.

## Recommended

*C. argentea* is the species from which both the **Cristata Group** (crested celosia) and **Plumosa Group** (plume celosia) were developed. Crested celosias have cockscomb, or brain-like, flowers and plume celosias have softer, plume-like flowers. Plants are bushy and often have leaves that are veined in the same color as the long-lasting flowers. Cultivars of both types are available. **'Fresh Look Red'** and **'Fresh Look Yellow'** are plume celosias with red or yellow flowers respectively and were 2004 All-America Selections winners. **'Prestige Scarlet'** is a 1997 All-America Selections winner. It is a crested celosia with vivid red blooms and bronzy purple-green foliage.

---

**Also called:** cockscomb **Features:** long-lasting, red, orange, purple, gold, yellow, pink, magenta flowers; bushy habit; sometimes colorful foliage **Height:** 10–36"
**Spread:** 10–36"

# Cleome

*Cleome*

Create a bold and exotic display in your garden with these lovely, unusual flowers, and watch these pretty plants as they sway in the wind.

## Growing

Cleome prefers **full sun** but tolerates partial shade. Plants adapt to most soils, though mixing in **organic matter** to help retain water is a good idea regardless of your soil conditions. These plants are drought tolerant but perform best when watered regularly. Pinch out the tip of the center stem on young plants to encourage branching and the production of more plentiful blooms. Deadhead to prolong blooming and reduce the prolific self-seeding.

## Tips

Cleome can be planted in groups at the back of a border or in the center of an island bed. This striking plant also makes an attractive addition to a large mixed container planting.

## Recommended

*C. hassleriana* is a tall, upright plant with strong, supple, hairy stems. The foliage and flowers of this plant have a strong but not unpleasant scent. Flowers are borne in loose, rounded clusters at the ends of the leafy stems. Many cultivars are available.

*C. spinosa* 'Sparkler Blush' is 2002 All-America Selections winner. It is a shorter selection—reaching a height of 3' when mature—making it suitable for small gardens and even container gardening.

C. hassleriana (above & below)

*This plant could also be given the name "hummingbird flower." Blooming through to fall, cleome provides nectar for the tiny birds after many other flowers have finished blooming.*

**Also called:** spider flower **Features:** attractive, scented foliage; purple, pink, white flowers; hairy stems **Height:** 3–5' **Spread:** 12–24"

# Cosmos
*Cosmos*

*C. bipinnatus* (above), *C. sulphureus* (below)

With their array of bright shades, cosmos flowers add a splash of bright color to any garden.

*Cosmos make lovely and long-lasting additions to cut-flower arrangements.*

## Growing

Cosmos prefer **full sun** and a **sheltered** location, out of the wind. The soil should be of **poor to average fertility** and **well drained**. These plants are drought tolerant, and too much water or fertilizer can reduce flowering. Sow seed directly into the garden in spring. Deadhead to encourage more flowering. Poke twiggy sticks into the ground around young seedlings to support the plants as they grow.

## Tips

Cosmos make an attractive addition to cottage gardens and the backs of borders. Try mass planting them in informal beds and borders.

## Recommended

*C. atrosanguineus* is an upright plant that grows 30" tall. It bears fragrant, dark maroon flowers that some gardeners claim smell a bit like chocolate.

*C. bipinnatus* is a tall plant with feathery foliage. It bears flowers in many shades of pink as well as red, purple, white and sometimes bicolored. Older cultivars grow 3–6' tall, whereas some of the newer varieties grow 12–36" tall. Many cultivars are available.

*C. sulphureus* (yellow cosmos) is an upright plant that bears flowers in shades of yellow, orange or red. Older cultivars grow up to 7' tall, whereas newer ones grow 1–4' tall. Many cultivars are available.

**Features:** pink, purple, red, white, yellow, orange, maroon flowers; feathery foliage
**Height:** 1–7' **Spread:** 12–18"

# Fan Flower

*Scaevola*

*F*an flower's intriguing one-sided flowers add interest to hanging baskets, planters and window boxes.

## Growing

Fan flower grows well in **full sun** or **light shade**. The soil should be of **average fertility, moist** and very **well drained**. Water regularly because this plant doesn't like to dry out completely. It does, however, recover quickly from wilting when watered.

## Tips

Fan flower is popular for hanging baskets and containers, but it can also be used along the tops of rock walls and in rock gardens where it will trail down. This plant makes an interesting addition to mixed borders, or it can be used under shrubs, where the long, trailing stems will form an attractive groundcover.

## Recommended

**S. aemula** forms a mound of foliage from which trailing stems emerge. The fan-shaped flowers come in shades of purple, usually with white bases. The species is rarely grown because there are many improved cultivars.

*Given the right conditions, this Australian plant will flower abundantly from April through to frost.*

*S. aemula* (above & below)

**Features:** unique blue or purple flowers; trailing habit **Height:** up to 8" **Spread:** 36" or more

# Geranium
*Pelargonium*

*P. zonale* cultivar (above), *P. peltatum* (below)

Tough, predictable, sun loving and drought resistant, geraniums have earned their place as flowering favorites in the annual garden. If you are looking for something out of the ordinary, seek out the scented geraniums with their fragrant and often decorative foliage.

## Growing

Geraniums prefer **full sun** but will tolerate partial shade, though they may not bloom as profusely. The soil should be **fertile** and **well drained**. Deadheading is essential to keep geraniums blooming and looking neat.

## Tips

Geraniums are very popular annual plants, and are used in borders, beds, planters, hanging baskets and window boxes. They are perennials that are treated as annuals, and they can be kept indoors over the winter in a bright room.

## Recommended

*P.* x *hortorum* 'Black Velvet Rose' is a 2002 All-America Selections winner. The dark-centered foliage with light green margins contrasts nicely with its light pink flowers.

*P. peltatum* (ivy-leaved geranium) has thick, waxy leaves and a trailing habit. Many cultivars are available.

*P. species* and **cultivars** (scented geraniums, scented pelargoniums) are a large group of geraniums that have fragrant leaves. The scents are grouped into categories including rose, mint, citrus, fruit, spice and pungent.

*P. zonale* (zonal geranium) is a bushy plant with red, pink, purple, orange or white flowers and, frequently, banded or multi-colored foliage. Many cultivars are available.

---

**Features:** colorful red, pink, violet, orange, salmon, white, purple flowers; decorative or scented foliage; variable habits
**Height:** 8–24"  **Spread:** 6"–4'

# Heliotrope
## *Heliotropium*

*A*new generation of gardeners has renewed the popularity of this old-fashioned favorite. Heliotrope's big clusters of fragrant flowers, bushy habit and deeply veined foliage are much admired.

### Growing
Heliotrope grows best in **full sun**. The soil should be **fertile, humus rich, moist** and **well drained**. Overwatering can kill heliotrope, but a plant that is allowed to dry out to the point of wilting recovers very slowly. This cold-sensitive plant should be set outside only after the danger of frost has passed. Cover heliotrope or bring it indoors if unseasonable frost is expected and before the first fall frost if you plan to overwinter it indoors.

### Tips
Heliotrope is ideal for growing in containers or flowerbeds near windows and patios, where the wonderful fragrance of the flowers can be enjoyed. It can also be grown indoors in a bright, sunny window.

### Recommended
*H. arborescens* is a low, bushy shrub that is treated as an annual. It produces large clusters of fragrant flowers in purple, blue or white. Many cultivars are available.

*H. arborescens* (above & below)

*Heliotrope kept a little on the dry side tends to have more strongly scented flowers, but a plant shouldn't be allowed to dry out for prolonged periods.*

---

**Also called:** cherry pie plant **Features:** fragrant, purple, blue, white flowers; attractive foliage **Height:** 18–24" **Spread:** 12–24"

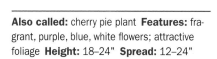

# Impatiens
*Impatiens*

*I. walleriana* (above), *I. hawkeri* (below)

For many years now, impatiens have been a staple in the shade garden, delivering masses of season-long flowers in a wide variety of colors.

## Growing

Impatiens do best in **partial or light shade** but tolerate full shade  If kept moist, they will tolerate full sun. In midsummer, impatiens in sunny locations may need daily watering. New Guinea impatiens are the best adapted to sunny locations. The soil should be **fertile, humus rich, moist** and **well drained**.

## Tips

Impatiens are known for their ability to grow and flower profusely even in shade.

Mass plant them in beds under trees, along shady fences or walls or in porch planters. They also look lovely in hanging baskets. New Guinea impatiens are grown as much for their variegated leaves as for their flowers.

## Recommended

*I. hawkeri* (New Guinea hybrids; New Guinea impatiens) has flowers in shades of red, orange, pink, purple or white. The foliage is often variegated with a yellow stripe down the center of each leaf.

*I. walleriana* (impatiens, busy Lizzie) has flowers in shades of purple, red, burgundy, pink, yellow, salmon, orange, apricot or white and can be bicolored. Dozens of cultivars are available.

**Also called:** busy Lizzie **Features:** colorful flowers in shades of purple, red, burgundy, pink, yellow, salmon, orange, apricot, white or bicolored flowers; grows well in shade **Height:** 6–36" **Spread:** 12–24"

# Lantana
*Lantana*

This low-maintenance plant, with its stunning flowers, thrives in hot weather and won't suffer if you forget to water it.

## Growing

Lantana grows best in **full sun** but tolerates partial shade. The soil should be **fertile, moist** and **well drained**. Plants are drought and heat tolerant. Cuttings can be taken in late summer and grown indoors for the winter so you will have plants the following year.

## Tips

Lantana makes an attractive addition to beds and borders as well as in mixed containers and hanging baskets.

*L. camara* is a tender, bushy shrub that is grown as an annual. It bears round clusters of flowers in a variety of colors. The blooms often change color as they mature, giving the flower clusters a striking, multi-colored appearance. Good examples of this are **'Feston Rose,'** which has flowers that open yellow and mature to bright pink, and **'Radiation,'** which bears flowers that open yellow and mature to red.

*L. camara* cultivar (above), *L. camara* 'Radiation' (below)

**Also called:** shrub verbena **Features:** stunning yellow, orange, pink, purple, red, white flowers; flower clusters often multi-colored **Height:** 18–24" **Spread:** up to 4'

# Madagascar Periwinkle
*Catharanthus*

*C. roseus* (above & below)

Madagascar periwinkle is a forgiving annual, tolerant of dry spells, searing sun and pollution. It exhibits grace under all types of pressure. Its lovely flowers are often mistaken for impatiens, and it is a good substitute for impatiens in hot, sunny, dry locations.

### Growing
Madagascar periwinkle prefers **full sun** but tolerates partial shade. Any **well-drained soil** is fine. This plant prefers to be watered regularly but doesn't like to be too wet or too cold. Don't plant seedlings out until the soil has warmed, because they may fail to thrive in cold, wet soil.

### Tips
Madagascar periwinkle does well in the sunniest, warmest part of the garden. Plant it in a bed along an exposed driveway or against the south-facing wall of the house. It can be used in hanging baskets, in planters and as a temporary groundcover.

### Recommended
*C. roseus* forms a mound of strong stems. The flowers are pink, red or white, often with contrasting colors. The following are All-America Selections winners: **'First Kiss Blueberry'** (2005), **'Jaio Dark Red'** (2003) and **'Jaio Scarlet Eye'** (2002). Many other cultivars are available.

**Also called:** vinca, annual vinca
**Features:** attractive foliage; flowers in shades of red, rose, mauve, white, often with contrasting centers; durable plants
**Height:** 6–24" **Spread:** equal to or greater than height

# Marigold
*Tagegetes*

From the large, exotic, ruffled flowers of African marigold to the tiny flowers of the low-growing signet marigold, the warm colors and fresh scent of these plants add a festive touch to the garden.

## Growing

Marigolds grow best in **full sun**. The soil should be of **average fertility** and **well drained**. These plants are drought tolerant and hold up well in windy, rainy weather. Sow seed directly in the garden after the chance of frost has passed. Deadhead to prolong blooming and to keep plants tidy.

## Tips

Mass planted or mixed with other plants, marigolds make a vibrant addition to beds, borders and container gardens. These plants will thrive in the hottest, driest parts of your garden.

## Recommended

There are many cultivars available for all of the species.

*T. erecta* (African marigold, American marigold) is the largest species with the biggest flowers.

*T. patula* (French marigold) is low growing and has a wide range of flower colors.

*T. tenuifolia* (signet marigold) has become more popular recently because of its feathery foliage and small, dainty flowers.

*T. patula* 'Boy Series' (above), *T. patula* hybrid (below)

*T.* **Triploid Hybrids** (triploid marigold) have been developed by crossing French and African marigolds, which results in plants that combine huge flowers with compact growth.

**Features:** brightly colored yellow, red, orange, brown, gold, cream, bicolored flowers; fragrant foliage **Height:** 6–36" **Spread:** 12–24"

# Melampodium
*Leucanthemum*

*L. paludosum* (above & below)

Melampodium is a lovely low-growing annual that gives a bright and cheery look to the garden with its small but lovely daisy-like yellow flowers. It is somewhat drought tolerant and is easy to maintain.

### Growing
Melampodium grows well in **full sun** or **partial shade**. The soil should be of **average fertility, moist** and **well drained**. Direct sow seeds in spring.

*These plants are native to Portugal and Spain and deserve to be used more frequently in the garden.*

### Tips
Melampodium makes a bright sunny addition to beds, borders and mixed container plantings. Plants can be arranged in small groups or mass planted as a groundcover to fill a larger space.

### Recommended
*L. paludosum (Melampodium paludosum)* forms a bushy mound of bright green foliage 2–6" tall. Bright yellow, daisy-like flowers are produced all summer. **'Medallion'** is larger than the species, growing up to 12" tall. **'Million Gold'** flowers more profusely than the species. **'Show Star'** has leaves with wavy edges and bright yellow flowers.

**Also called:** butter daisy, medallion flower
**Features:** bright yellow flowers
**Height:** 2–12"  **Spread:** 6–12"

# Nasturtium

*Tropaeolum*

These plants have fast-growing, brightly colored flowers and are easy to grow. For these reasons, they are popular with beginner and experienced gardeners alike.

## Growing
Nasturtiums prefer **full sun** but tolerate some shade. The soil should be of **poor to average fertility, light, moist** and **well drained**. Soil that is too rich or has too much nitrogen fertilizer will result in lots of leaves and very few flowers. Let the soil drain completely between waterings. Sow directly in the garden once the danger of frost has passed.

## Tips
Nasturtiums are used in beds, borders, containers and hanging baskets as well as on sloped banks. The climbing varieties are grown up trellises or over rock walls or places that need concealing. These plants thrive in poor locations, and they make interesting additions to plantings on hard-to-mow slopes.

## Recommended
*T. majus* has a trailing habit, but many of the cultivars have bushier, more refined habits. Cultivars offer differing flower colors or variegated foliage.

*T. majus* (above), *T. majus* cultivar (below)

*These lovely flowering plants add color, dimension and depth to the garden.*

**Features:** brightly colored red, orange, yellow, burgundy, pink, cream, gold, white, bicolored flowers; attractive foliage; edible flowers and leaves; varied habits **Height:** 12–18" for dwarf varieties; up to 10' for trailing varieties **Spread:** equal to height

# Nicotiana
*Nicotiana*

N. x *sanderae* cultivar (above & below)

Nicotianas were originally culti-vated for the wonderful fragrance of the flowers. With more recent variet-ies, the fragrance has sometimes been lost in favor of an expanded selection of flower colors, but fragrant varieties are still available.

### Growing
Nicotianas grow equally well in **full sun, light shade or partial shade**. The soil should be **fertile, high in organic matter, moist** and **well drained**.

### Tips
Nicotianas are popular in beds and borders. The dwarf selec-tions do well in mixed containers.

Do not plant nicotianas near tomatoes because they are mem-bers of the same plant family and share a vulnerability to many of the same diseases. Nicotianas can attract and harbor diseases that will modestly affect them but can kill your tomatoes.

### Recommended
*N. x sanderae* (*N. alata* x *N. forgetiana*) is a bushy, upright plant with slightly fuzzy leaves that feel almost sticky to the touch. Plants range in size from dwarfs 12–18" tall to taller plants that reach 5' in height. **'Avalon Bright Pink'** is a 2001 All-America Selections winner. It is a dwarf nicotiana with lovely pink, star-shaped flowers. **'Perfume Deep Purple'** is a 2006 All-America Selections winner with a fragrance that is most noticable during the evening hours.

*The seeds require light to germinate, so if you start plants from seed, press them into the soil surface but don't cover them.*

**Also called:** flowering tobacco
**Features:** fragrant red, pink, green, yellow, white, purple flowers **Height:** 1–5'
**Spread:** 12"

# Pansy
*Viola*

*V. x wittrockiana* (above & below)

Colorful and cheerful, pansy flowers are a welcome sight in spring after a long, dreary winter.

## Growing

Pansies prefer **full sun,** but tolerate partial shade. The soil should be **fertile, moist** and **well drained.** Pansies do best when the weather is cool, and they often die back in the summer heat. They may rejuvenate in late summer, but you will generally get a better display if you pull up faded plants and replace them with new ones in fall. These plants may very well survive winter and provide you with flowers again in spring. Should the winter be on the mild side, some pansies will grace the dormant landscape with flowers.

## Tips

Pansies can be used in beds and borders, and they are popular mixed in with spring-flowering bulbs and primroses. They can also be grown in containers.

## Recommended

*V. cornuta* **'Skippy XL Red-Gold'** is a 2006 All-America Selections winner. Its flowers are ruby red with violet shading and whiskery markings below the golden yellow face. It has larger flowers than most plants of this species.

*V. x wittrockiana* is a small, bushy plant that bears flowers in a wide range of bright and pastel colors, often with markings near the centers of the petals that give the flowers a facelike appearance.

**Also called:** viola **Features:** colorful flowers in bright or pastel shades of blue, purple, red, orange, yellow, pink, white; flowers often bicolored **Height:** 6–12" **Spread:** 6–12"

# Parrot Leaf
*Alternanthera*

A. *ficoidea* (above)

Parrot leaf is a colorful, bronzy, low-growing annual that is suitable for lining garden borders.

### Growing
Parrot leaf develops the best leaf color when grown in **full sun**, but it tolerates partial shade. The soil should be of **average fertility** and **well drained,** but this plant adapts to most soil conditions. Pinch tips or shear lightly to encourage bushy growth.

*These brightly colored perennials are native to Mexico and South America and can be brought indoors for the winter. A few cuttings in late summer will provide you with an attractive houseplant that will grow happily in a sunny window.*

### Tips
Parrot leaf is an excellent plant for edging formal beds and can be mass planted in borders or used as an annual groundcover. Include it in mixed container plantings or dot small groups throughout your garden to add bright splashes of color here and there.

### Recommended
*A. ficoidea* is a bushy, rounded perennial that is treated like an annual. It has insignificant flowers and is grown for the brightly variegated leaves of the cultivars. The green or bronze leaves of the cultivars are marked with red, pink, purple, orange or yellow.

**Also called:** Joseph's coat **Features:** green or bronze leaves with red, pink, yellow, purple or orange markings **Height:** 6–12" **Spread:** 12" or more

# Petunia
*Petunia*

For speedy growth, prolific season-long blooming and ease of care, petunias are hard to beat.

## Growing

Petunias prefer **full sun**. The soil should be of **average to rich fertility, light, sandy** and **well drained**. To encourage new growth and flowers, pinch some varieties in mid-summer.

## Tips

Use petunias in beds, borders, containers and hanging baskets.

## Recommended

*P.* x *hybrida* is a large group of popular, sun-loving annuals that fall into three categories. **Grandifloras** have the largest flowers in the widest range of colors, but they can be damaged by rain. **Multifloras** bear more flowers that are smaller and less easily damaged by heavy rain. **Millifloras** are the least common with the smallest flowers in the narrowest range of colors, but they are the most prolific and least likely to be damaged by heavy rain. Two popular multiflora cultivars that are All-America Selections winners are **'Lavender Wave,'** a spreading, trailing plant that bears light purple flowers all summer, and **'Tidal Wave Silver,'** which is a bushy, spreading plant that bears silvery white flowers with pinky purple veining. A number of petunias are All-America Selections winners.

P. multiflora type (above & below)

*Because of the introduction of many new and exciting cultivars, petunias are once again among the most popular and sought after of the annual garden flowers.*

**Features:** colorful pink, purple, red, white, yellow, coral, blue, bicolored flowers; versatile plants **Height:** 6–18" **Spread:** 12–24" or wider

# Poppy
*Papaver*

P. somniferum 'Peony Flowered' (above)
P. nudicaule (below)

Poppies seem to have been made to grow in groups. The many flowers swaying in the breeze with their often curving stems almost appear to be having lively conversations with one another.

## Growing

Poppies grow best in **full sun**. The soil should be **fertile** and **sandy** with lots of **organic matter** mixed in. Good drainage is essential. Direct sow seeds every two weeks in spring by mixing the tiny seeds with fine sand for even sowing. Do not cover the seeds because they need light for germination. Deadhead to prolong blooming.

## Tips

Poppies work well in mixed borders where other plants grow slower. They fill in empty spaces early in the season, then die back over the summer, leaving room for other plants. They can also be used in rock gardens, and the cut flowers are popular for fresh arrangements.

## Recommended

*P. nudicaule* (Iceland poppy) bears red, orange, yellow, pink or white flowers in spring and early summer.

*P. rhoeas* (Flanders poppy, field poppy, corn poppy) forms a basal rosette of foliage above which the flowers, in a wide range of colors, are borne on long stems.

*P. somniferum* (opium poppy) bears red, pink, white or purple, often showy, single or double flowers. Although propagation of the species is restricted in many countries because of its narcotic properties, several attractive cultivars have been developed for ornamental use.

*Be careful when weeding around faded summer plants; you may accidentally pull up late-summer poppy seedlings.*

**Also called:** Shirley poppy, corn poppy, Flanders poppy **Features:** brightly colored red, pink, white, purple, yellow, orange flowers **Height:** 2–4' **Spread:** 12"

# Portulaca
*Portulaca*

For a brilliant show in the hottest, driest, poorest, most neglected area of the garden, you can't go wrong with portulaca.

## Growing
Portulaca requires **full sun**. The soil should be of **poor fertility, sandy** and **well drained**. To ensure that you will have plants where you want them, start the seeds indoors. If you sow directly outdoors, the tiny seeds may get washed away by rain, resulting in the plants popping up in unexpected places.

## Tips
Portulaca is the ideal plant for garden spots that just don't get enough water— under the eaves of the house or in dry, rocky, exposed areas. It is also ideal for people who like baskets hanging from the front porch but forget to water regularly. This plant will still need to be watered occasionally, but as long as the location is sunny, portulaca will do well with minimal care.

## Recommended
*P. grandiflora* forms a bushy mound of succulent foliage. Its delicate, papery, rose-like flowers are produced profusely all summer. Many cultivars are available, including some with flowers that stay open on cloudy days. **'Margarita Rosita'** is a 2001 All-America Selections winner. Its double, rose-like flowers, which bloom throughout the growing season, make it stand out from other portulacas.

*P. grandiflora* (above & below)

*Spacing the plants close together is not a problem; in fact, the intertwining of the plants and colorful flowers creates an interesting and attractive effect.*

**Features:** colorful, drought-resistant summer flowers in shades of red, pink, yellow, white, purple, orange, peach **Height:** 4–8" **Spread:** 6–12" or wider

# Sage
*Salvia*

S. splendens (above), S. farinacea 'Victoria' (below)

Sage should be part of every annual garden. The attractive and varied forms have something to offer every style of garden.

*There are over 900 species of* Salvia.

## Growing

All sage plants prefer **full sun** but will tolerate light shade. The soil should be **moist, well drained** and of **average to rich fertility,** with lots of **organic matter.** To keep plants producing flowers, water them often and fertilize monthly.

## Tips

Sage looks great grouped in beds, borders and containers. Circles, squares and other shapes lend themselves to be filled in with sage plants. The long-lasting flowers make good cut flowers for arrangements.

## Recommended

*S. argentea* (silver sage) is grown for its large, fuzzy, silvery leaves.

*S. coccinea* (Texas sage) is a bushy, upright plant that bears whorled spikes of white, pink, blue or purple flowers.

*S. farinacea* (mealy cup sage, blue sage) has bright blue flowers clustered along stems powdered with silver. Cultivars are available including **'Evolution,'** a 2006 All-America Selections winner with bright violet summer flowers.

*S. splendens* (salvia, scarlet sage) is grown for its spikes of bright red, tubular flowers. Cultivars have recently become available with white, pink, purple or orange flowers.

*S. viridis* (S. horminium; annual clary sage) is grown for its colorful pink, purple, blue or white bracts, rather than the tiny flowers within the bracts.

**Also called:** salvia **Features:** colorful red, blue, purple, burgundy, pink, orange, salmon, yellow, cream, white, bicolored, summer flowers; attractive foliage **Height:** 8"–4' **Spread:** 8"–4'

# Snapdragon
*Antirrhinum*

Snapdragons are among the most appealing plants. The flower colors are always rich and vibrant, and even the most jaded gardeners are tempted to squeeze open the dragons' mouths.

## Growing

Snapdragons prefer **full sun** but tolerate light or partial shade. The soil should be **fertile, rich in organic matter** and **well drained**. These plants prefer a **neutral or alkaline soil** and will not perform as well in acidic soil. Do not cover seeds when sowing because they require light for germination.

Pinch the tips of the young plants to encourage bushy growth. Cut off the flower spikes as they fade to promote further blooming and to prevent the plant from dying back before the end of the season.

## Tips

The height of the variety dictates the best place for it in a border—the shortest varieties work well near the front, and the tallest look great in the center or at the back. The dwarf and medium-height varieties can also be used in planters. A trailing variety does well in hanging baskets.

## Recommended

Many cultivars of **A. majus** are available, generally grouped into three size categories: dwarf, medium and giant. Plants are bushy in habit and bear several spikes of colorful flowers from early or mid-summer to fall.

*A. majus* cultivar (above & below)

*Snapdragons are perennial plants that are treated like annuals. Though they won't usually survive the winter here, they will often flower well into fall and may self-seed.*

**Features:** entertaining and colorful white, cream, yellow, orange, red, maroon, pink, purple, bicolored flowers **Height:** 6"–4' **Spread:** 6–24"

# Sunflower
*Helianthus*

*E*ach of the many sunflower options adds cheerful charm to any garden.

### Growing
Sunflower grows best in **full sun**. The soil should be of **average fertility, humus rich, moist** and **well drained**. Successive sowings from spring to early summer prolong the blooming period.

The annual sunflower is an excellent flower for a child's garden. The seeds are big and easy to handle and they germinate quickly. Until the flower finally appears on top, the plants grow continually upward, and their progress can be measured.

### Tips
Low-growing varieties can be used in beds, borders and containers. Tall varieties work well at the back of borders and make good screens and temporary hedges. The tallest varieties may need staking.

*H. annuus* 'Teddy Bear' (above)
*H. annuus* cultivar (below)

### Recommended
*H. annuus* has attractive cultivars in a wide range of heights, with single stems or branching habits. The flowers come in a variety of colors, in single to fully double forms. **'Ring of Fire'** is a 2002 All-America Selections winner. Its 5" diameter blossoms are gold or yellow.

**Also called:** common sunflower
**Features:** late-summer, single or double flowers with yellow, orange, red, brown, cream or bicolored petals and contrasting brown, purple or rusty red centers; edible seeds
**Height:** 12–24" for dwarfs; up to 15' for giants **Spread:** 12–36"

# Sweet Alyssum
## *Lobularia*

*L. maritima* cultivars (above & below)

Sweet alyssum is excellent for creating soft edges. As a bonus, it self-seeds, popping up along pathways and between stones late in the season, giving summer a sweet sendoff.

### Growing
Sweet alyssum prefers **full sun** but tolerates light shade. **Well-drained soil** of **average fertility** is preferred, but poor soil is tolerated. Sweet alyssum may die back a bit during the heat and humidity of summer. Trim the plants back and water them periodically in summer to encourage new growth and more flowers when the weather cools.

### Tips
Sweet alyssum creeps around rock gardens, billows over rock walls and fills the edges of beds and containers. It can be seeded into cracks and crevices of walkways and between patio stones. Once established, it readily reseeds. It is also good for filling in spaces between taller plants in borders and mixed containers.

### Recommended
***L. maritima*** forms a low, spreading mound of foliage. The entire plant appears to be covered in tiny, fragrant blossoms when in full flower. Cultivars with flowers in a wide range of colors are available.

*Leave alyssum plants in the garden over the winter. In spring, remove the previous year's growth to expose the self-sown seedlings beneath.*

---

**Also called:** alyssum **Features:** fragrant flowers in pink, white, purple, yellow, salmon **Height:** 3–12" **Spread:** 6–24"

# Verbena
*Verbena*

V erbenas offer a banquet to
butterflies, including tiger
swallowtails, silver-spotted skip-
pers, great spangled fritillaries
and painted ladies.

### Growing
Verbenas grow best in **full sun**.
The soil should be **fertile** and very
**well drained**. Pinch back young
plants for bushy growth.

### Tips
Use verbenas on rock walls and
in beds, borders, rock gardens,
containers, hanging baskets and
window boxes. They make good
substitutes for ivy-leaved geranium where the sun is hot and
where a roof overhang keeps the
mildew-prone verbenas dry.

### Recommended
*V. bonariensis* forms a low clump
of foliage from which tall, stiff
stems bear clusters of small, purple flowers.

*V. x hybrida* is a bushy plant that
may be upright or spreading. It
bears clusters of small flowers in
a wide range of colors. Cultivars
are available.

*V. bonariensis (above), V. x hybrida (below)*

*V. canadensis 'Homestead Purple' is a
popular perennial species of verbena. It is
a low, spreading plant with glossy leaves
that grows about 18" tall. It bears purple
flowers in summer.*

**Also called:** garden verbena
**Features:** colorful red, pink, purple, blue,
yellow, scarlet, silver, peach, white flowers,
some with white centers **Height:** 8"–5'
**Spread:** 12–36"

# Zinnia
*Zinnia*

*Z*innias are popular in gardens and flower arrangements, adding much-needed color to the late-summer and fall garden.

## Growing
Zinnias grow best in **full sun**. The soil should be **fertile, humus rich, moist** and **well drained**. To avoid disturbing the roots when transplanting seedlings, start the seeds in individual peat pots. Deadhead to prolong blooming and keep plants looking neat.

## Tips
Zinnias are useful in beds, borders, containers and cutting gardens. The dwarf selections can be used as edging plants. These plants provide wonderful fall color.

## Recommended
*Z. angustifolia* (narrow-leaf zinnia) is a low, mounding, mildew-resistant plant that bears yellow or orange flowers. Plants grow 6–12" tall. **'Crystal White'** bears white flowers.

*Z. elegans* is a bushy, upright plant with daisy-like flowers in a variety of forms and colors. Heights vary from 6–36". Many cultivars are available including 2006 All-America Selections winner **'Zowie! Yellow Flame,'** a mildew-resistant selection that grows 24" tall. The flowers have deep pink and scarlet petal bases with yellow tips.

*Z.* **Profusion Series** are compact, mildew-resistant hybrids that grow 10–18" tall and bear flowers in bright cherry red,

Z. Profusion Series 'Profusion White' (above)
Z. elegans 'Zowie! Yellow Flame' (below)

orange or white. The individual cultivars are named for the flower colors; **'Profusion Cherry,' 'Profusion Orange'** and **'Profusion White'** are All-America Selections winners.

---

**Features:** bushy plants; flowers in shades of red, yellow, green, purple, orange, pink, white, maroon, brown, gold; some are bicolored or tricolored **Height:** 6–36" **Spread:** 12–18"

# Anemone

*Anemone*

*A. x hybrida* (above & below)

As the rest of the garden begins to fade in late summer, anemone is just beginning its fall show. The white and pink flowers are a welcome sight in the fall garden, which is usually dominated by yellow and orange.

*There are many more species of anemone available, including several lovely low-growing, spring-flowering selections.*

## Growing

Anemone prefers **partial or light shade** but tolerates full sun. The soil should be **average to fertile, humus rich** and **moist**. Anemone is not drought tolerant and therefore needs to be watered when rainfall is lacking. The soil should, however, be allowed to dry out while plants are dormant to prevent root rot. Mulching around plants for the first winter can help the plants become established. Don't mulch over the crown, though.

## Tips

Anemones make beautiful additions to lightly shaded borders, woodland gardens and cottage gardens.

## Recommended

*A. hupehensis* var. *japonica* (Japanese anemone) is an upright plant with dark green leaves. It bears lovely light pink flowers in late summer and fall. It grows 2–4' tall and spreads 18". Cultivars with flowers in varied shades of pink are available.

*A. x hybrida* is an upright plant with a suckering habit. It grows 4–5' tall and spreads about 24". Flowers in shades of pink or white are produced in late summer and early fall. Many cultivars are available.

**Also called:** Japanese anemone, windflower
**Features:** pink or white flowers in late summer and fall **Height:** 2–5' **Spread:** 18–24"
**Hardiness:** zones 4–8

# Aster

*Aster*

Fall just isn't fall without the blossoms of beautiful asters, which often provide a last meal for migrating butterflies. The purples and pinks of asters make a nice contrast to the yellow-flowered perennials common in the late-summer garden.

## Growing

Asters prefer **full sun** but tolerate partial shade. The soil should be **fertile, moist** and **well drained**. Pinch or shear these plants back in early summer to promote dense growth and reduce disease problems. Mulch in winter to protect plants from temperature fluctuations. Divide every two to three years to maintain vigor and control spreading.

## Tips

Use asters in the middle of borders and in cottage gardens, or naturalize them in wild gardens.

## Recommended

Some aster species have been reclassified under the genus *Symphyotrichum*. You may see both names at garden centers.

*A. novae-angliae* (New England aster) is an upright, spreading, clump-forming perennial that generally bears yellow-centered, purple flowers. Many cultivars are available with flowers in other colors.

*A. novi-belgii* (Michaelmas daisy, New York aster) is a dense, upright, clump-forming perennial generally with purple flowers. Many cultivars are available with flowers in other colors.

A. novae-angliae (above), A. novi-belgii (below)

*What looks like a single flower of an aster, or other plant with daisy-like flowers, is actually a cluster of many tiny flowers. Look closely at the center of a flower and you will see all the individual florets.*

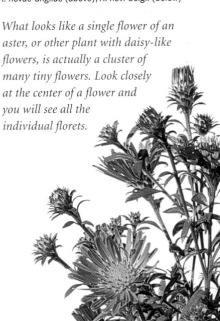

**Features:** late summer to mid-fall flowers in shades of red, white, blue, purple or pink, often with yellow centers **Height:** 10"–5' **Spread:** 18–36" **Hardiness:** zones 4–8

# Astilbe

*Astilbe*

A. x *arendsii* cultivars (above)
A. x *arendsii* 'Bressingham Beauty' (below)

Astilbes are beacons in the shade. Their high-impact, plume-like flowers will brighten any gloomy section of your garden.

*In late summer, transplant seedlings found near the parent plant to create plumes of color all through the garden.*

## Growing

Astilbes grow best in **light or partial shade** and tolerate full shade, though they will not flower as much. They also tolerate full sun if the soil is kept consistently moist. The soil should be **fertile, humus rich, acidic, moist** and **well drained**. Although these plants appreciate moist soil, they don't like standing water.

Astilbe should be divided every three years or so to maintain plant vigor. Root masses may lift out of the soil as they mature. Add a layer of topsoil and mulch if this occurs.

## Tips

Astilbes can be grown near the edges of bog gardens and ponds or in woodland gardens and lightly shaded borders.

## Recommended

**A. x *arendsii*** (astilbe, false spirea, Arend's astilbe) is a group of hybrids with many available cultivars Plants are similar in appearance to the other two species.

**A. chinensis** (Chinese astilbe) is a dense, vigorous perennial that tolerates dry soil better than other astilbe species. Many cultivars are available.

**A. japonica** (Japanese astilbe) is a compact, clump-forming perennial. The species is rarely grown in favor of the many cultivars.

**Features:** attractive foliage; white, pink, purple, peach, red, summer flowers
**Height:** 10"–4'  **Spread:** 8–36"
**Hardiness:** zones 3–9

# Bellflower
## *Campanula*

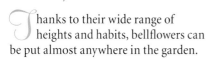

Thanks to their wide range of heights and habits, bellflowers can be put almost anywhere in the garden.

## Growing

Bellflowers grow well in **full sun, partial shade or light shade**. The soil should be of **average to high fertility** and **well drained**. These plants appreciate a mulch to keep their roots cool and moist in summer and protected in winter, particularly if snow cover is inconsistent. Deadhead to prolong blooming.

## Tips

Plant upright and mounding bellflowers in borders and cottage gardens. Use low, spreading and trailing bellflowers in rock gardens and on rock walls. You can also edge beds with the low-growing varieties.

## Recommended

*C.* x **'Birch Hybrid'** is a low-growing and spreading plant. It bears light blue to mauve flowers in summer.

*C. carpatica* (Carpathian bellflower, Carpathian harebell) is a clump-forming perennial that bears blue, white or purple flowers in summer. Several cultivars are available.

*C. glomerata* (clustered bellflower) forms a clump of upright stems and bears clusters of purple, blue or white flowers throughout most of the summer.

*C. persicifolia* (peach-leaved bellflower) is an upright perennial that bears white, blue or purple flowers from early summer to mid-summer.

*C. persicifolia* (above), *C. carpatica* 'White Clips' (below)

*C. poscharskyana* is a trailing perennial that likes to wind its way around other plants. It bears light violet-blue flowers in summer and early fall.

Also called: campanula  Features: blue, white, purple, pink, spring, summer or fall flowers; varied growing habits  Height: 4"–6' Spread: 12–36"  Hardiness: zones 3–7

# Blazing Star
*Liatris*

With fuzzy, spiked blossoms above grass-like foliage, blazing star makes an outstanding cut flower. It is also an excellent plant for attracting butterflies to the garden.

## Growing

Blazing star prefers **full sun**. The soil should be of **average fertility, sandy** and **humus rich**. Water well during the growing season, but don't allow the plant to stand in water during cool weather. Plant it in a location that has good drainage to avoid root rot in winter. Mulch during summer to prevent moisture loss.

Trim off the spent flower spikes to promote a longer blooming period and to keep blazing star looking tidy. Divide every three or four years in fall. The clump will appear crowded when it is time to divide.

*L. spicata* 'Kobold' (above), *L. spicata* (below)

## Tips

Use this plant in borders and meadow plantings. Blazing star also grows well in planters.

## Recommended

*L. spicata* is a clump-forming, erect plant. The flowers are pinkish purple or white. Several cultivars are available.

*The flower spikes of blazing star are unique in their blooming sequence. They bloom from top to bottom rather than the more common bottom to top flowering.*

**Also called:** spike gayfeather, gayfeather
**Features:** purple or white, summer flowers; grass-like foliage **Height:** 18–36"
**Spread:** 18–24" **Hardiness:** zones 3–9

# Bleeding Heart
## *Dicentra*

Every garden should have a spot for the bleeding heart plant. Tucked away in a shady spot, this lovely plant appears in spring and fills the garden with fresh promise.

## Growing

Bleeding hearts prefer **light shade** but tolerate partial or full shade. The soil should be **humus rich, moist** and **well drained**. Very dry summer conditions cause the plants to die back, though they will revive in fall or the following spring. Bleeding hearts must remain moist while blooming to prolong the flowering period. Regular watering will keep the flowers coming until mid-summer.

## Tips

Bleeding hearts can be naturalized in a woodland garden or grown in a border or rock garden. They make excellent early-season specimen plants and do well near ponds or streams.

## Recommended

**D. eximia** (fringed bleeding heart) forms a loose, mounded clump of lacy, fern-like foliage and bears pink or white flowers in spring and sporadically over the summer.

**D. formosa** (western bleeding heart) is a low-growing, wide-spreading plant with pink flowers that fade to white as they mature. The most drought tolerant of the bleeding hearts, it is the most likely to continue flowering all summer.

**D. spectabilis** (common bleeding heart, Japanese bleeding heart) forms a large,

*D. formosa (above), D. spectabilis (below)*

elegant mound that bears flowers with white inner petals and pink outer petals. Several cultivars are available.

*All bleeding hearts contain toxic alkaloids, and some people develop allergic skin reactions from contact with these plants.*

**Features:** pink, white, red, purple, spring and summer flowers; attractive foliage
**Height:** 1–4'  **Spread:** 12–36"
**Hardiness:** zones 3–9

# Chrysanthemum

*Chrysanthemum*

*C.* x *morifolium* hybrid (above & below)

Perk up your fall garden with a bright display of fall mums, with their masses of colorful flowers.

## Growing

Chrysanthemums grow best in **full sun**. The soil should be **fertile, moist** and **well drained**. Plant as early in the growing season as possible to increase the chances that chrysanthemums will survive the winter. Pinch plants back in early summer to encourage bushy growth and increase flower production.

Divide plants every two or three years to keep them growing vigorously.

## Tips

Chrysanthemums in the fall garden provide a blaze of color that lasts right until the first hard frost. In groups or as specimen plants they can be included in borders, in planters or in plantings close to the house. Purchased in fall, they can be added to spots where summer annuals have faded.

## Recommended

*C.* **Hybrids** form a diverse group of plant series with varied hardiness in New York. A few popular hybrids are found in the **Prophet Series**. It includes cultivars with flowers in a wide range of colors including '**Christine,**' with deep salmon pink flowers and '**Raquel,**' with bright red flowers.

**Features:** late summer or fall flowers in shades of orange, red, yellow, pink, red, purple; habit **Height:** 12–36" **Spread:** 2–4' **Hardiness:** zones 5–9

# Columbine

## *Aquilegia*

Delicate and beautiful columbines add a touch of simple elegance to any garden. Blooming from the cool of spring through to mid-summer, these long-lasting flowers herald the passing of spring and the arrival of warm summer weather.

## Growing

Columbines grow well in **light or partial shade.** They prefer soil that is **fertile, moist** and **well drained,** but they adapt to most soil conditions. Division is not required but can be done to propagate desirable plants. The divided plants may take a while to recover because columbines dislike having their roots disturbed.

## Tips

Use columbines in rock gardens, in formal or casual borders and in naturalized or woodland gardens.

## Recommended

*A. canadensis* (wild columbine, Canada columbine) is a native plant that is common in woodlands and fields. It bears yellow flowers with red spurs.

*A. x hybrida* (*A.* x *cultorum;* hybrid columbine) forms mounds of delicate foliage and has exceptional flowers. Many hybrids have been developed with showy flowers in a wide range of colors.

*A. vulgaris* (European columbine, common columbine, granny's bonnet) has been used to develop many hybrids and cultivars with flowers in a variety of colors.

**Features:** red, yellow, pink, purple, blue, white, spring and summer flowers; color of spurs often differs from that of petals; attractive foliage **Height:** 18–36" **Spread:** 12–24" **Hardiness:** zones 3–9

*A. canadensis* (above)
*A. x hybrida* 'McKana Giants' (below)

*Columbines self-seed but are not invasive. Each year, a few new seedlings may turn up near the parent plant and you can transplant them.*

# Coreopsis
*Coreopsis*

*C. verticillata* 'Moonbeam' (above), *C. verticillata* (below)

These easy-to-grow plants produce flowers all summer long and make a fabulous addition to every garden.

## Growing

Coreopsis grows best in **full sun**. The soil should be of **average fertility, sandy, light** and **well drained**. Too fertile a soil will encourage floppy growth. Plants can develop crown rot in moist, cool locations with heavy soil, and most varieties can withstand short periods of drought. Deadhead to keep plants blooming.

## Tips

Coreopsis are versatile plants, useful in formal and informal borders and in meadow plantings and cottage gardens. They look best when planted in groups.

## Recommended

*C. verticillata* (thread-leaf coreopsis) is a mound-forming plant with attractive, finely divided foliage and bright yellow flowers. Available cultivars include the 1992 Perennial Plant of the Year, **'Moonbeam,'** which forms a mound of delicate, lacy foliage and bears creamy yellow flowers.

*Deadheading such a vigorous-blooming plant can be a big job. Most gardeners simply use garden shears to trim the spent flowers off, taking a few of the current blooms off at the same time. Plants recover quickly with a new flush of blooms.*

**Also called:** tickseed **Features:** yellow to yellow-orange, summer flowers; attractive foliage **Height:** 24–36" **Spread:** 18–24" **Hardiness:** zones 3–9

# Daylily

*Hemerocallis*

*H.* 'Stella de Oro' (above), *H.* 'Bonanza' (below)

The daylily's adaptability and durability combined with its variety in color, blooming period, size and texture explain this perennial's popularity.

## Growing

Daylilies grow in any light from **full sun** to **full shade**. The deeper the shade, the fewer the flowers produced. The soil should be **fertile, moist** and **well drained,** but these plants adapt to most conditions and are hard to kill once established. Daylilies can be left indefinitely without dividing, but it's nice to divide them every two to three years to keep them vigorous and propagate them.

## Tips

Plant daylilies alone or group them in borders, on banks and in ditches to control erosion. They can be naturalized in woodland or meadow gardens. Small varieties are nice in planters.

## Recommended

Daylilies come in an almost infinite number of forms, sizes and colors in a daunting range of species, cultivars and hybrids. Visit your local garden center or daylily grower to find out what's available. Ask for field-grown daylilies; they seem to establish most quickly in the garden.

*Deadhead these plants to prolong the blooming period. Be warned that when deadheading purple-flowered daylilies, the sap can stain fingers and clothes.*

**Features:** spring and summer flowers in every color except blue and pure white; grass-like foliage **Height:** 1–4' **Spread:** 1–4'
**Hardiness:** zones 2–9

# Epimedium

*Epimedium*

*E. grandiflorum* 'Rubinkrone' (above)
*E.* x *rubrum* (below)

*L*ong-lived and low maintenance, with attractive, heart-shaped, often colorful foliage and delicate sprays of orchid-like flowers, this plant is a woodland garden favorite.

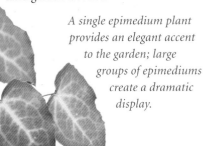

*A single epimedium plant provides an elegant accent to the garden; large groups of epimediums create a dramatic display.*

### Growing

Epimedium grows best in **light or partial shade** but tolerates full shade. The soil should be **average to fertile, humus rich** and **moist,** though plants are fairly drought tolerant once established. Cut back the foliage, especially if it's tattered, before new growth begins in spring.

### Tips

These spring-blooming plants are popular in shade and woodland gardens, as accent plants or as groundcovers. They can be planted under taller, shade-providing plants in beds and borders as well as in moist, pondside plantings. Epimedium can be slow to establish, but it's worth the wait.

### Recommended

Many species, hybrids and cultivars are available.

*E.* x *cantabrigiense* is a clump-forming plant with dark green leaves and flowers that are pink-beige and yellow.

*E. grandiflorum* is also a clump-forming plant. Its cultivars have large, delicate, creamy white to dark pink flowers.

*E.* x *perralchicum* 'Frohnleiten' is a Long Island Gold Medal Award winner. It is a compact, spreading plant that quickly establishes and is relatively maintenance free. Its bright yellow flowers and reddish green foliage persist into winter.

*E.* x *rubrum* is a low-spreading plant with small, wine and cream colored flowers.

**Also called:** barrenwort, bishop's hat
**Features:** yellow, orange, cream, white, pink, red, purple, spring flowers; foliage; habit
**Height:** 6–18" **Spread:** 12–24"
**Hardiness:** zones 4–8

# Foxglove
## *Digitalis*

*D. purpurea* (above & below)

Foxgloves are perfect foils for the members of the daisy family that are so common in the summer landscape.

## Growing
Foxgloves grow well in **partial or light shade**. The soil should be **fertile, humus rich, acidic** and **moist**. Start seeds in mid- to late summer for blooms the following summer, or purchase plants in spring for blooms the summer they are planted. Plants often self-seed, and they may pop up in your garden in future summers.

## Tips
Foxgloves are must-haves for the cottage garden and for gardeners interested in heritage plants. They make excellent vertical accents along the back of a border and are attractive additions to woodland gardens.

## Recommended
***D. purpurea*** forms a mounding basal rosette of foliage from which the tall flower spikes emerge. Plants bloom in early summer with flowers in a wide range of colors, often with contrasting speckles on the insides of the flowers. There are many cultivars and hybrids available.

*All parts of this plant are poisonous; wear gloves when handling plants and wash your hands thoroughly afterwards.*

**Also called:** purple foxglove **Features:** pink, yellow, purple, maroon, red, white, early-summer flowers; habit **Height:** 2–5' **Spread:** 12–24" **Hardiness:** zones 4–8

# Goat's Beard

*Aruncus*

*A. dioicus* (above & below)

*Male and female flowers are produced on separate plants. In general, male flowers are full and fuzzy and female flowers are more pendulous, but it can be difficult to tell the two apart.*

Despite its imposing size, goat's beard has a soft and delicate appearance with its divided foliage and large, plume-like, cream-colored flowers.

### Growing

Goat's beards prefer **partial to full shade**. If planted in deep shade, they bear fewer blooms. They tolerate some full sun as long as the soil is kept evenly moist and they are protected from the afternoon sun. The soil should be **fertile, moist** and **humus rich**.

### Tips

These plants look very natural growing near the sunny entrance or edge of a woodland garden, in a native plant garden or in a large island planting. They may also be used in a border or alongside a stream or pond.

### Recommended

**A. aethusifolius** (dwarf Korean goat's beard) forms a low-growing, compact mound and bears branched spikes of loosely held, cream flowers.

**A. dioicus** (giant goat's beard, common goat's beard) forms a large, bushy, shrub-like perennial with large plumes of creamy white flowers. There are several cultivars.

---

**Features:** cream or white early to mid-summer blooms; shrub-like habit; attractive foliage and seedheads **Height:** 6"–6' **Spread:** 1–6' **Hardiness:** zones 3–7

# Hardy Geranium

*Geranium*

The geraniums often thought of as annuals are in the genus *Pelargonium;* the genus *Geranium* is better known for its vast selection of lovely flowering perennials. There is a style of geranium for every garden, thanks to the beauty and diversity of this hardy plant.

## Growing

Hardy geraniums grow well in **full sun, partial shade or light shade**. These plants dislike hot weather and prefer soil of **average fertility** with **good drainage**. *G. renardii* prefers a poor, well-drained soil. Divide in spring.

## Tips

These long-flowering plants are great in a border; they fill in the spaces between shrubs and other larger plants, and they keep the weeds down. Include geraniums in rock gardens and woodland gardens, or mass plant them as groundcovers.

## Recommended

**G. macrorrhizum** (bigroot geranium, scented cranesbill) forms a spreading mound of fragrant foliage and bears flowers in shades of pink and purplish pink. Cultivars are available.

**G. renardii** (Renard's geranium) forms a clump of velvety, deeply veined, crinkled foliage. A few purple-veined white flowers appear over the summer, but the foliage remains the main attraction.

*G. sanguineum* var. *striatum* (above)
*G. sanguineum* (below)

**G. sanguineum** (bloody cranesbill) forms a dense, mounding clump and bears bright magenta flowers. Many cultivars are available.

*If the foliage tatters in late summer, prune it back to rejuvenate it.*

---

**Also called:** cranesbill geranium
**Features:** white, red, pink, purple, blue, summer flowers; attractive, sometimes fragrant, foliage **Height:** 4–36" **Spread:** 12–36"
**Hardiness:** zones 3–8

# Hosta

*Hosta*

H. sieboldiana 'Elegans' (above)

## Growing

Hostas prefer **light or partial shade** but will grow in full shade. Morning sun is preferred over afternoon sun in partial shade situations. The soil should ideally be **fertile, moist** and **well drained,** but most soils are tolerated. Hostas are moderately drought tolerant, especially if given a mulch to help retain moisture. Marginal browning will occur during prolonged periods of drought. Division is not required but can be done every few years in spring or summer to propagate new plants.

## Tips

Hostas make wonderful woodland plants and look very attractive when combined with ferns and other fine-textured plants. Hostas also work well in a mixed border, particularly when used to hide the ugly, leggy lower stems and branches of some shrubs. The dense growth and thick, shade-providing leaves suppress weeds.

Breeders are always seeking new variations in the foliage of shade-loving hostas. Swirls, stripes, puckers and ribs enhance the leaves' various sizes, shapes and colors.

## Recommended

Hostas have been subjected to a great deal of crossbreeding and hybridizing, resulting in hundreds of cultivars. Visit your local garden center or get a mail-order catalogue to find out what's available.

**Also called:** plantain lily **Features:** decorative foliage; white or purple, summer and fall flowers **Height:** 4–36" **Spread:** 6"–6' **Hardiness:** zones 3–8

*[handwritten: PHYSOSTEGIA L4.99 Pinky mauve  Solidago yellow]*

# Iris

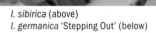
*Iris*

Irises are steeped in history and lore. Many gardeners say the range in flower colors of bearded irises approximates that of a rainbow.

## Growing

Irises prefer **full sun** but tolerate very light or dappled shade. The soil should be of **average fertility** and **well drained**. Japanese irises and Siberian irises prefer a moist, well-drained soil. Deadhead irises to keep them tidy, and divide in late summer or early fall. Cut back the foliage of Siberian iris in spring.

## Tips

All irises are popular border plants, but Japanese irises and Siberian irises are also useful alongside streams or ponds. Dwarf cultivars make attractive additions to rock gardens.

## Recommended

There are many iris species and hybrids available. Among the most popular are the bearded irises, often hybrids of **I. germanica**. They have the widest range of flower colors but are susceptible to attack from iris borers, which can kill the plants. Several species of irises are not susceptible to these pests, including Japanese iris (**I. ensata**) and Siberian iris (**I. sibirica**). Check with your local garden center to find out what's available.

*I. sibirica* (above)
*I. germanica* 'Stepping Out' (below)

*Wash your hands after handling irises because they can cause severe internal irritation if ingested.*

**Features:** spring, summer and sometimes fall flowers in many shades of pink, red, purple, blue, white, brown, yellow; attractive foliage
**Height:** 4"–4' **Spread:** 6"–4'
**Hardiness:** zones 3–10

# Lamb's Ears

*Stachys*

*S. byzantina* 'Big Ears' (above), *S. byzantina* (below)

This plant's soft, fuzzy leaves are reminiscent of a lamb's ears, hence its name. The foliage creates a textural delight in the garden.

## Growing

Lamb's ears grows best in **full sun**. The soil should be of **poor to average fertility** and **well drained**. The leaves can rot in humid weather if the soil is poorly drained.

Deadhead to keep plants looking neat or select a flowerless cultivar. Cut plants with withered or damaged foliage back to 3–5" in spring or after flowering, and fresh, new foliage will flourish.

## Tips

Lamb's ears makes a great groundcover in a garden with soil that has not yet been amended. Use it to edge borders and pathways, where it will provide a soft, silvery backdrop for more vibrant colors. For a silvery accent, plant a small group of lamb's ears.

## Recommended

*S. byzantina* (*S. olympica*) forms a mat of thick, woolly rosettes of leaves. Pinkish purple flowers are produced all summer long. **'Helen von Stein'** ('Big Ears'; Helene Von Stein lamb's ears) is a Long Island Gold Medal Award winner. It has greenish silver leaves that are twice as large as those of the species. This clump-forming perennial groundcover occasionally produces flower spikes. It is deer and pest resistant. **'Silver Carpet'** has silvery white, fuzzy foliage. Both of these cultivars rarely produce flowers.

**Also called:** woolly betony **Features:** pink or purple, summer flowers; decorative foliage **Height:** 6–18" **Spread:** 18–24" **Hardiness:** zones 3–8

# Lavender
*Lavandula*

Lavender is considered the queen of herbs. With both aromatic and ornamental qualities, it makes a valuable addition to any garden.

## Growing

Lavenders grow best in **full sun** but tolerate light shade. The soil should be **average to fertile** and **alkaline,** and it must be **well drained**. Once established, these plants are heat and drought tolerant. Protect plants from winter cold and wind. In colder areas, lavenders should receive additional mulching and with luck, a good layer of snow. Plants can be sheared in spring or after flowering.

## Tips

Lavenders are wonderful, aromatic edging plants. They can be planted in drifts or as specimens in small spaces, or they can be used to form a low hedge.

## Recommended

*L. angustifolia* (English lavender) is an aromatic, bushy subshrub. It grows up to about 24" tall with an equal spread. From mid-summer to fall, it bears spikes of small, light purple flowers. Many cultivars are available, including selections with white or pink flowers, silvery gray to olive green foliage and dwarf or compact habits.

*L.* **x** *intermedia* (lavandin) is a natural hybrid between English lavender and spike lavender (*L. latifolia*). It grows 36" tall with an equal spread. The flowers are held on long spikes. Cultivars are available.

*L. angustifolia* (above & below)

Features: purple, pink, blue, white, mid-summer to fall flowers; fragrance; evergreen foliage; habit Height: 8–36" Spread: up to 4' Hardiness: zones 5–9

# Meadowsweet

*Filipendula*

F. ulmaria 'Variegata' (above), F. ulmaria (below)

*Deadhead meadowsweets if you desire, but the faded seedheads are quite attractive when left in place.*

For an impressive, informal, vertical accent and showy clusters of fluffy, fragrant flowers, meadowsweet plants are second to none.

## Growing

Meadowsweets prefer **partial or light shade,** but they tolerate full sun if the soil remains sufficiently moist. The soil should be **fertile, deep, humus rich** and **moist,** except in the case of *F. vulgaris,* which prefers dry soil. Divide in spring or fall.

## Tips

Most meadowsweets are excellent plants for bog gardens or wet sites. Grow them alongside streams or in moist meadows. Meadowsweets may also be grown in the back of a border, as long as they are kept well watered. Grow *F. vulgaris* if you can't provide the moisture needed by the other species.

## Recommended

*F. rubra* (queen-of-the-prairie) forms a large, spreading clump and bears clusters of fragrant, pink flowers. Cultivars are available.

*F. ulmaria* (queen-of-the-meadow) forms a mounding clump and bears creamy white flowers in large clusters. Cultivars are available.

*F. vulgaris* (dropwort, meadowsweet) is a low-growing species that bears clusters of fragrant, creamy white flowers. Cultivars with double or pink flowers, or with variegated foliage are available.

**Features:** white, cream, pink, red, late-spring or summer flowers; attractive foliage
**Height:** 2–8'  **Spread:** 18"–4'
**Hardiness:** zones 3–8

# Peony
## *Paeonia*

From the simple single flowers to the extravagant doubles, it's easy to become mesmerized with these voluptuous plants. Once the fleeting, but magnificent, flower display is done, the foliage remains stellar throughout the growing season.

## Growing

Peonies prefer **full sun** but tolerate some shade. The planting site should be well prepared before the plants are introduced. Peonies like **fertile, humus-rich, moist, well-drained soil,** to which lots of compost has been added. Mulch peonies lightly with compost in spring. Too much fertilizer, particularly nitrogen, causes floppy growth and retards blooming. Division is not required but can be done in fall to propagate plants. Deadhead to keep plants looking tidy.

Planting depth determines whether or not a peony will flower. Tubers planted too shallow or, more commonly, too deep, will not flower. The buds or eyes on the tuber should be 1–2" below the soil surface.

## Tips

These wonderful plants look great in a border combined with other early bloomers. They can be planted close to bulbs and other plants that die down by mid-summer—the emerging foliage of the peonies will hide the dying foliage of the spring bloomers. Avoid planting peonies under trees, where they will have to compete for light, moisture and nutrients.

*P. lactiflora* 'Shimmering Velvet' (above)
*P. lactiflora* cultivars (below)

Place peony cages around the plants in early spring to support the heavy flowers. The foliage will grow up into the wires and hide the cage.

## Recommended

There are hundreds of peonies available. Cultivars come in a wide range of colors, may have single or double flowers, and may or may not be fragrant. Visit your local garden center to see what is available.

**Features:** white, cream white, yellow, pink, red, purple, spring and early-summer flowers; attractive foliage **Height:** 24–32" **Spread:** 24–32" **Hardiness:** zones 2–7

# Pinks

*Dianthus*

*Gentiana
pink & blue 22.99*

D. deltoides (above), D. plumarius (below)

From tiny and delicate to large and robust, this genus contains a wide variety of plants, many with spice-scented flowers.

## Growing

Pinks prefer **full sun** but tolerate some light shade. A **well-drained, neutral or alkaline soil** is required. The most important factor in the successful cultivation of pinks is **good drainage**—they hate to stand in water. Rocky outcroppings make up the native habitat of many species of pinks.

## Tips

Pinks make excellent plants for rock gardens and rock walls, and for edging flower borders and walkways. They can also be used in cutting gardens and even as groundcovers. To prolong blooming, deadhead as the flowers fade, but leave a few flowers in place to go to seed.

## Recommended

*D. chinensis* 'Corona Cherry Magic' was an All-America Selections winner for 2003. This plant is compact, but it bears large, variable, light and dark pink flowers, from solid cherry pink to light pink with cherry red centers.

*D. deltoides* (maiden pinks) forms a mat of foliage and flowers in shades of red, pink and white. Cultivars are available.

*D. gratianopolitanus* (cheddar pinks) is long-lived and forms a very dense mat of evergreen, silver gray foliage with sweet-scented flowers mostly in shades of pink. 'Firewitch' forms a compact hummock of silvery pink foliage, which provides a striking contrast to its deep pink flowers. This cultivar was named Perennial Plant of the Year for 2006. Other cultivars are also available.

*D. plumarius* (cottage pinks) is noteworthy for its role in the development of many popular cultivars known collectively as garden pinks. The flowers can be single, semi-double or fully double and are available in many colors.

**Features:** sometimes fragrant, pink, red, white, purple, spring or summer flowers; attractive foliage and habit **Height:** 2–18" **Spread:** 6–24" **Hardiness:** zones 3–9

# Plumbago
*Ceratostigma*

C. *plumbaginoides* (above & below)

Plumbago is a tough plant that spreads nicely to fill in any shady or sunny spot it is offered.

## Growing

Grow plumbago in **full sun** or **partial shade**—it will not bloom in full shade. The soil should be **average to fertile** and **well drained**. Plants are fairly drought tolerant once established. Remove any tattered or winter-damaged leaves and growth in spring before the new growth begins. Plants that die back completely in winter may be difficult to spot in spring. Avoid disturbing the plants in spring because they are late to emerge.

## Tips

This plant is useful on exposed banks where mowing is impossible or undesirable. Plumbago also makes a wonderful addition to a rock garden. It creeps happily between the rocks of a stone wall.

## Recommended

*C. plumbaginoides* is a low, mounding, spreading plant. It bears bright blue flowers in late summer. The foliage turns an attractive bronzy red in fall.

**Also called:** dwarf plumbago, leadwort
**Features:** bright blue, late-summer flowers; habit; foliage; fall color  **Height:** 10–18"
**Spread:** 12–18" or more
**Hardiness:** zones 5–9

# Purple Coneflower
*Echinacea*

*E. purpurea* (above & below)

As interest in this plant has grown, plant breeders have sought out uncommon species and have developed many exciting new cultivars and hybrids.

## Growing

Purple coneflower grows well in **full sun** or **very light shade**. It tolerates any well-drained soil, but prefers an **average to rich soil**. This plant is drought resistant, but it prefers to have regular water. Divide every four years or so in spring or fall.

Deadhead early in the flowering season to prolong blooming. Later, leave the flowerheads in place to self-seed and provide winter interest. Pinch plants back or thin out the stems in early summer to encourage bushy growth that is less prone to mildew.

## Tips

Use purple coneflower in meadow gardens and informal borders, either in groups or as single specimens.

## Recommended

Many species, cultivars and hybrids are available in a wide range of plant sizes and with daisy-like flowers in many colors.

*E.* **'Double Decker'** has deep rose-colored flowers. Out of the central cone grows a second set of petals, producing a madcap effect. *E.* **'Harvest Moon'** has golden yellow petals around an orangy yellow center. *E.* Orange Meadowbright ('Art's Pride') bears deep orange flowers with reddish orange centers. *E. purpurea* has prickly hairs all over. It bears purple flowers with orangy centers. **'Kim's Knee High'** is a popular, low-growing bushy cultivar. *E.* **'Twilight'** bears dark pink flowers with striking red centers.

**Also called:** coneflower, echinacea
**Features:** purple, pink, white, yellow, orange, mid-summer to fall flowers with rusty orange centers; persistent seedheads
**Height:** 18"–5' **Spread:** 12–24"
**Hardiness:** zones 3–8

# Russian Sage

*Perovskia*

*P. atriplicifolia* (above), *P. atriplicifolia* 'Filigran' (below)

Russian sage offers four-season interest in the garden: soft, gray-green leaves on light gray stems in spring; fuzzy, violet-blue flowers in summer and silvery white stems in fall that last until late winter.

## Growing

Russian sage prefers **full sun**. The soil should be **poor to moderately fertile** and **well drained**. Too much water and nitrogen will cause this plant's growth to flop, so do not plant it next to heavy feeders. Russian sage cannot be divided because it is a subshrub that originates from a single stem. In spring, when new growth appears low on the branches, or in fall, cut the plant back hard to about 6–12" to encourage vigorous, bushy growth.

## Tips

The silvery foliage and blue flowers work well with other plants in the back of a mixed border and soften the appearance of daylilies. Russian sage can also create a soft screen in a natural garden or on a dry bank.

## Recommended

*P. atriplicifolia* is a loose, upright plant with silvery white, finely divided foliage. The small, lavender blue flowers are loosely held on silvery, branched stems. Cultivars are available.

**Features:** blue or purple, mid-summer to fall flowers; attractive habit; fragrant, gray-green foliage **Height:** 3–4' **Spread:** 3–4'
**Hardiness:** zones 5–9

# Sedum

*Sedum*

S. *spurium* 'Dragon's Blood' (above)
S. 'Autumn Joy' (right)

Some 300 to 500 species of sedum are distributed throughout the Northern Hemisphere. Many sedums are grown for their foliage, which can range in color from steel gray-blue and green to red and burgundy.

## Growing

Sedums prefer **full sun** but tolerate partial shade. The soil should be of **average fertility,** very **well drained** and **neutral to alkaline.** Divide in spring when needed.

*Early-summer pruning of upright species and hybrids encourages compact, bushy growth but can delay flowering.*

## Tips

Low-growing sedums make wonderful groundcovers and additions to rock gardens or rock walls. They also edge beds and borders beautifully. Taller sedums give a lovely late-season display in a bed or border.

## Recommended

*S.* **'Autumn Joy'** (autumn joy sedum) is a popular upright hybrid. The flowers open pink or red and later fade to deep bronze. This hybrid is extremely drought tolerant.

*S. spectabile* (showy stonecrop) is an upright species with pink flowers. Cultivars are available.

*S. spurium* (two-row stonecrop) forms a low, wide mat of foliage with deep pink or white flowers. Many cultivars are available and are often grown for their colorful foliage.

---

**Also called:** stonecrop **Features:** yellow, white, red, pink, summer to fall flowers; decorative fleshy foliage **Height:** 2–24"
**Spread:** 12–24" or more
**Hardiness:** zones 3–8

# Shasta Daisy
## *Leucanthemum*

*L. x superbum* (above & below)

These old-fashioned, long-blooming beauties never go out of style.

## Growing

Shasta daisies grow well in **full sun** or **partial shade**. The soil should be **fertile, moist** and **well drained**. Plants may be short-lived in hardiness zones 4 and 5. Pinch plants back in late spring or early summer to encourage compact, bushy growth. Deadheading extends the blooming period by several weeks.

## Tips

Use this plant in perennial and mixed borders where it can be grown as a single plant or massed in groups. The flowers can be cut for fresh flower arrangements.

**L. x superbum** forms a large clump of dark green leaves and stems. It bears large, white, daisy-like flowers with bright yellow centers all summer and often until the first frost. **'Becky'** is a Long Island Gold Medal Award winner. It grows about 36" tall and bears many flowers. With deadheading, this shasta daisy flowers for most of the summer. It is pest resistant, drought and heat tolerant and is almost maintenance free.

*This classic perennial daisy lends itself well to the "loves me, loves me not" game played by children and the lovesick.*

---

**Features:** yellow-centered, white, daisy-like, summer flowers; habit **Height:** 1–4'
**Spread:** about 24" **Hardiness:** zones 4–10

# Vinca
*Vinca*

Vinca grows well in a wide range of soils and welcomes spring with a bounty of blue flowers.

## Growing

Vinca grows well in **partial to full shade. Moist, well-drained soil** of any type will do. After planting, mulch the soil with shredded leaves and compost to keep the soil moist and to prevent weeds from sprouting up while vinca fills in.

## Tips

Vinca is a useful and attractive groundcover in a shrub border, under trees or on a shady bank. It is shallow-rooted and can outcompete weeds without interfering with deeper-rooted shrubs. Shear plants back in early spring if they begin to outgrow their space.

*V. minor* (above & below)

## Recommended

***V. minor*** forms a low, loose mat of trailing stems. Purple or blue flowers are borne in a flush in spring and sporadically throughout the summer. Many cultivars are available, with different-colored flowers or variegated foliage.

*The Romans used the long, trailing stems of the vinca plant to make wreaths. This use of the plant may explain its name, which is derived from the Latin* vincire, *"to bind."*

**Also called:** myrtle, lesser periwinkle
**Features:** blue, purple, white, red, mid-spring to fall flowers; trailing habit; evergreen foliage
**Height:** 4–8" **Spread:** indefinite
**Hardiness:** zones 4–8

# Yarrow

*Achillea*

Yarrows are informal, tough plants with a fantastic range of flower colors.

## Growing

Yarrows grow best in **full sun**. The soil should be of **average fertility, sandy** and **well drained**. These plants tolerate drought and poor soil. They will also tolerate heavy, wet soil and humidity, but they do not thrive in such conditions. Excessively rich soil or too much nitrogen results in weak, floppy growth.

Divide every two or three years in spring. Deadhead to prolong blooming. Basal foliage should be left in place over the winter and tidied up in spring.

## Tips

Cottage gardens, wildflower gardens and mixed borders are perfect places for these informal plants. They thrive in hot, dry locations where nothing else will grow.

## Recommended

**A. filipendulina** forms a clump of ferny foliage and bears yellow flowers. It has been used to develop several hybrids and cultivars.

**A. millefolium** (common yarrow) forms a clump of soft, finely divided foliage and bears white flowers. Many cultivars exist, with flowers in a wide range of colors.

*A. millefolium* 'Paprika' (above)
*A. filipendulina* (below)

*Yarrows make excellent groundcovers. They send up shoots and flowers from a low basal point and may be mowed periodically without excessive damage to the plant. Mower blades should be kept at least 4" high.*

**Features:** white, yellow, red, orange, pink, purple, mid-summer to early-fall flowers; attractive foliage; spreading habit **Height:** 4"–4' **Spread:** 12–36" **Hardiness:** zones 3–9

# Atlas Cedar
*Cedrus*

*C. atlantica* 'Glauca Pendula' (above), *C. atlantica* 'Glauca' (below)

These elegant trees, with their towering forms and sweeping, layered branches, are a sight to behold.

## Growing

Atlas cedar grows well in **full sun** and **partial shade**. The soil should be **average to fertile, loamy, moist** and **well drained,** though these plants adapt to most soils.

## Tips

Smaller cultivars are available, but generally cedars are very large and are best suited to larger properties and park-like settings. These trees are hardy only in the warmer parts of New York State.

## Recommended

*C. atlantica* is a pyramidal or conical tree with an open habit and elegant, ground-sweeping branches. It generally grows 40–60' tall, though up to 100' is possible. It spreads up to 40'. **'Glauca'** (f. *glauca;* blue Atlas cedar) has stunning silvery to blue-green needles and is a magnificent, eye-catching tree. It grows as big as the species. **'Glauca Pendula'** is a weeping form with blue-green needles that is staked when it is young to develop a central leader from which the branches can cascade. It will grow only as tall as the central leader is staked.

*This tree is native to the Atlas Mountains of Morocco and Algeria.*

**Features:** large, upright, spreading or pendulous, evergreen conifer with green, blue or silvery needles, upright cones and fissured, silvery bark **Height:** 40–60' **Spread:** 30–40' **Hardiness:** zones 6–9

# Barberry
### *Berberis*

*T*he variations available in plant size, foliage color, flowers and fruit make barberry a real workhorse of the plant world.

## Growing
Barberry develops the best fall color when grown in **full sun,** but it tolerates partial shade. Any **well-drained soil** is suitable. This plant tolerates drought and urban conditions but suffers in poorly drained, wet soil.

## Tips
Large barberry plants make great barriers and security hedges with their formidable prickles. Barberry can also be included in shrub and mixed borders. Small cultivars can be grown in rock gardens, in raised beds and along rock walls.

## Recommended
*B. thunbergii* (Japanese barberry) is a dense deciduous shrub with a broad, rounded habit. The foliage is bright green and turns variable shades of orange, red or purple in fall. Yellow, spring or early-summer flowers are followed by glossy red fruit later in the summer. Many cultivars have been developed for their variable foliage color, including shades of purple and yellow as well as variegated selections. **'Helmond Pillar'** is an exceptionally narrow, upright selection, and **'Concorde'** is a dwarf selection with deep purple foliage.

*B. thunbergii* 'Helmond Pillar' (above)
*B. thunbergii* cultivar (below)

**Features:** prickly, deciduous shrub with attractive foliage; yellow flowers; glossy red fruit **Height:** 1–6' **Spread:** 18"–6'
**Hardiness:** zones 4–8

# Beautyberry
*Callicarpa*

*C. japonica* (above), *C. dichotoma* 'Early Amethyst' (below)

This florists' favorite adds pizzazz to your fall garden. Even though plants tend to die back in winter in the colder parts of New York, they dependably produce a stunning display of purple fruit every fall.

## Growing

Beautyberry grows well in **full sun** or **light shade**. The soil should be of **average fertility** and **well drained**. These shrubs may die back completely if the winter is cold enough. Fresh growth will emerge from the roots in spring and you will still get a good display of fruit as the plant blooms on new wood. Prune back dead branches in spring as the new growth is just emerging.

## Tips

Beautyberries can be used in naturalistic gardens and in shrub and mixed borders, where the uniquely colored fruit will add interest and contrast. The fruit-covered branches are often cut for fresh or dried arrangements because the colorful fruit persists on the branches.

## Recommended

*C. dichotoma* (purple beautyberry) is a bushy, upright shrub with arching clusters of purple fruit in fall. It grows 3–4' tall, with an equal or slightly greater spread.

*C. japonica* (Japanese beautyberry) is a large, open shrub with arching branches and decorative, purple fruit in fall. It can grow up to 10' tall but usually only grows 4' if it is killed back each winter. The plant can spread 4–6'. A white-fruited cultivar called **'Leucocarpa'** is available.

**Features:** bushy, deciduous shrub with arching stems that bear decorative, late-summer or fall fruit **Height:** 3–10' **Spread:** 3–6' **Hardiness:** zones 5–10

# Beech

*Fagus*

Beeches are large, boldly elegant shade trees that command a focal point in the landscape.

## Growing

Beeches grow equally well in **full sun** or **partial shade**. The soil should be of **average fertility, loamy** and **well drained,** though almost all well-drained soils are tolerated.

Beeches should be transplanted only when very young. American beech doesn't like having its roots disturbed or covered over. European beech transplants more easily and is more tolerant of varied soil conditions than American beech is.

## Tips

Beeches make excellent specimens. They are also used as shade trees and in woodland gardens. These trees need a lot of space, but the European beech's adaptability to pruning makes it a reasonable choice in a small garden if you are willing and able to prune it.

## Recommended

*F. grandifolia* (American beech) is a broad-canopied tree native to most of eastern North America. It can grow 50–70' in height and graces the fall landscape with its golden bronze foliage.

*F. sylvatica* (European beech) is a spectacular broad tree with a number of interesting cultivars. Several are small enough to use in the home garden, from

*F. grandifolia* (above), *F. sylvatica* (below)

narrow columnar and weeping varieties to varieties with purple or yellow leaves or pink, white and green variegated foliage.

*Plant a beech tree to celebrate the birth of children; it will still be there when they are adults and have their own children.*

**Features:** large, oval, deciduous shade tree; foliage; bark; habit; fall color; fruit
**Height:** 30–80'  **Spread:** 10–65'
**Hardiness:** zones 4–9

# Butterfly Bush
*Buddleia*

*B. davidii (above & below)*

This attractive deciduous bush with its fragrant flowers will attract countless beautiful and colorful butterflies along with a wide variety of other pollinating insects. Every garden should have a butterfly bush.

*Do not spray butterfly bushes and surrounding plants with pesticides because they will harm the butterflies as well as the beneficial insects.*

## Growing

Butterfly bushes prefer to grow in **full sun,** producing few, if any, flowers in shady conditions. The soil should be **fertile to average** and **well drained**. Plants are drought tolerant once established. Blooms form on the current year's growth, so even if plants are killed back during a particularly cold winter, they will still produce a fine display of flowers.

## Tips

Butterfly bushes make beautiful additions to shrub and mixed borders. Their graceful, arching habit makes them ideal as specimen plants. The dwarf forms are suitable for small gardens.

## Recommended

*B. davidii* (orange-eye butterfly bush, summer lilac) is the most commonly grown species. It grows 4–10' tall, with an equal spread. It bears fragrant flowers in bright and pastel shades of purple, pink, blue or white from mid-summer through fall. Many cultivars are available.

*B. x weyeriana* is a wide-spreading shrub with arching stems. It grows 6–12' tall, spreads 5–10' and bears purple or yellow flowers from mid-summer through fall. Cultivars are available. This species is hardy only to zone 6.

**Features:** large, deciduous shrub with arching branches; attractive flowers, habit and foliage **Height:** 4–12' **Spread:** 4–10' **Hardiness:** zones 5–9

# Caryopteris

*Caryopteris*

Caryopteris is a beautiful deciduous shrub that is cultivated for its aromatic stems, foliage and flowers. Its lovely blue flowers adorn the mid- and late-summer landscape. Bees just love this plant.

## Growing

Caryopteris prefers **full sun,** but it tolerates light shade. It does best in soil of **average fertility** that is **light** and **well drained.** Caryopteris is very drought tolerant once established, and wet, poorly drained soils can kill this plant. Treat it as a herbaceous perennial if growth is regularly killed back over the winter.

## Tips

Include caryopteris in your shrub or mixed border. The bright blue, late-season flowers are welcome when many other plants are past their flowering best.

## Recommended

**C. x clandonensis** forms a dense mound up to 36" tall and 3–5' in spread. It bears clusters of blue or purple flowers in late summer and early fall. Cultivars are available and are grown more often than the species.

C. x *clandonensis* cultivar (above)
C. x *clandonensis* (below)

**Also called:** bluebeard, blue spirea
**Features:** rounded, spreading, deciduous shrub; attractive, fragrant foliage, twigs and late-summer flowers **Height:** 2–4'
**Spread:** 2–5' **Hardiness:** zones 5–9

# Cedar
*Thuja*

T. occidentalis 'Sherwood Moss' (above)
T. occidentalis (below)

Cedars are rot resistant, durable and long-lived, earning quiet admiration from gardeners everywhere, plus they provide great privacy screening.

### Growing
Cedars prefer **full sun** but tolerate light to partial shade. The soil should be of **average fertility, moist** and **well drained**. These plants enjoy humidity and in the wild are often found growing near marshy areas. Cedars perform best in a location with some **shelter** from wind, especially in winter, when the foliage can easily dry out and give the entire plant a rather brown, drab appearance.

### Tips
Large varieties of cedars make excellent specimen trees, and smaller cultivars can be used in foundation plantings and shrub borders and as formal or informal hedges.

### Recommended
*T. occidentalis* (eastern arborvitae, eastern white cedar) is a narrow, pyramidal tree with scale-like, evergreen needles. There are dozens of cultivars available including shrubby dwarf varieties, varieties with yellow foliage and smaller, upright varieties. (Zones 2–7; some cultivars may be less cold hardy)

*T. plicata* (western arborvitae, western redcedar) is a narrow, pyramidal evergreen tree that grows quickly, resists deer browsing and maintains good foliage color all winter. It is also a Long Island Gold Medal Award winner. A number of cultivars are available including several dwarf varieties and a yellow-and-green-variegated variety. (Zones 5–9)

**Also called:** arborvitae **Features:** small to large, evergreen shrub or tree; foliage; bark; form **Height:** 2–50' **Spread:** 2–20' **Hardiness:** zones 2–9

# Cotoneaster

*Cotoneaster*

*C. dammeri* (above & below)

With their diverse sizes, shapes, flowers, fruit and foliage, cotoneasters are so versatile that they have many uses in the landscape.

## Growing

Cotoneasters grow well in **full sun** or **partial shade**. The soil should be of **average fertility** and **well drained**.

## Tips

Cotoneasters can be included in shrub or mixed borders. Low spreaders work well as groundcover, and shrubby species can be used to form hedges. Larger species are grown as small specimen trees and some low growers are grafted onto standards and grown as small, weeping trees.

## Recommended

Cotoneaster comes in many forms. *C. adpressus* (creeping cotoneaster) and *C. horizontalis* (rockspray cotoneaster) are low-growing groundcover plants. *C. apiculatus* (cranberry cotoneaster) and *C. dammeri* (bearberry cotoneaster) are wide-spreading, low, shrubby plants. *C. salicifolius* (willowleaf cotoneaster) is an upright shrubby plant that can be trained to form a small tree. These are just a few possibilities; your local garden center will be able to help you find a suitable tree for your garden.

*Cotoneaster berries can cause stomach upset if eaten.*

---

**Features:** evergreen or deciduous groundcover, shrub or small tree; foliage; early-summer flowers; persistent fruit; variety of forms
**Height:** 6"–15' **Spread:** 3–12'
**Hardiness:** zones 4–9

# Crabapple
*Malus*

M. 'Dolgo' (above)

*P*ure white through deep pink flowers, heights between 5' and 30' with similar spreads, tolerance of winter's extreme cold and summer's baking heat, and yellow through candy apple red fruit often persisting through winter—what more could anyone ask from a tree?

## Growing

Crabapples prefer **full sun** but will tolerate partial shade. The soil should be of **average to rich fertility, moist** and **well drained**. These trees tolerate damp soil.

One of the best ways to prevent the spread of crabapple pests and diseases is to clean up all the leaves and fruit that fall off the tree. Many pests overwinter in the fruit, leaves or soil at the base of the tree. Clearing away their winter shelter helps control pest populations.

## Tips

Crabapples make excellent specimen plants. Many varieties are quite small, so there is a form to suit almost any size of garden. Some forms are even small enough to grow in large containers. Crabapples' flexible young branches make these trees good choices for creating espalier specimens along a wall or fence.

## Recommended

Hundreds of crabapples are available. When choosing a species, variety or cultivar, look first for its disease resistance. Even the most beautiful flowers, fruit or habit will never look good if the plant is ravaged by pests or diseases. Ask for information about new, resistant cultivars at your local nursery or garden center. One popular cultivar with good disease resistance is SUGAR TYME, with pale pink buds that open to fragrant, white flowers and bright red fruit.

---

**Features:** rounded, mounded or spreading, small to medium, deciduous tree; spring flowers; late-season and winter fruit; fall foliage; habit; bark **Height:** 5–30' **Spread:** 6–30' **Hardiness:** zones 4–8

# Daphne
## *Daphne*

*D. x transaltantica* 'Jim's Pride' (above)

Daphne is a unique shrub that offers lovely fragrant flowers and interesting foliage.

### Growing
Daphne prefers **partial shade** and tolerates full sun well. The soil should be of **average fertility, moist** and **well drained**. A layer of mulch will keep the shallow roots cool. Avoid overfertilizing and overwatering.

### Tips
Include daphnes in shrub or mixed borders near paths, doors, windows or other places where their wonderful scent can be enjoyed.

### Recommended
*D.* x *transatlantica* 'Jim's Pride' (*D. caucasica*) is a Long Island Gold Medal Award winner. It is a rounded, upright, semi-evergreen to evergreen shrub. It bears clusters of fragrant, white flowers in late spring and until the first frost. Don't be surprised if you see some blossoms on warm winter days. Its attractive gray-green leaves are an added bonus.

*Be careful to keep children away from this plant, because all parts (including the seeds) are poisonous.*

**Features:** rounded, semi-evergreen to evergreen shrub; fragrant, white flowers all season long **Height:** 4–5' **Spread:** 4–5' **Hardiness:** zones 5–9

# Dogwood
*Cornus*

*C. alba* 'Bailhalo' (above), *C. kousa* var. *chinensis* (below)

Stem color, leaf variegation, fall color, growth habit, soil adaptability and hardiness are all positive attributes to be found in the dogwoods.

## Growing
Dogwoods grow equally well in **full sun, light shade or partial shade,** with a slight preference for light shade. The soil should be **average to fertile, humus rich, neutral to slightly acidic** and **well drained.**

## Tips
Shrub dogwoods can be included in a shrub or mixed border and look best in groups. The tree species make wonderful specimen plants and are small enough to include in most gardens. Use them along the edge of a woodland, in a shrub or mixed border, alongside a house or near a water feature.

## Recommended
*C. alba* (red-twig dogwood) and *C. sericea* (*C. stolonifera;* red-osier dogwood) are grown for their bright red, orange or yellow stems, which provide winter interest especially against a snowy background. Fall foliage color can also be attractive. (Zones 2–7)

*C. alternifolia* (pagoda dogwood) can be grown as a large, multi-stemmed shrub or a small, single-stemmed tree with attractively layered branches. Clusters of small, white flowers appear in early summer. (Zones 3–8)

*C. kousa* (Kousa dogwood) is grown for its flowers, fruit, fall color and interesting bark. The white-bracted flowers make a magnificent display, and they are followed by bright red fruit. The foliage turns red and purple in fall. **Var.** *chinensis* (Chinese dogwood) grows more vigorously and has larger flowers. (Zones 5–9)

**Features:** deciduous, large shrub or small tree; late-spring to early-summer flowers; fall foliage; stem color; fruit; habit **Height:** 5–30' **Spread:** 5–30' **Hardiness:** zones 2–9

# False Cypress
*Chamaecyparis*

*C. obtusa* 'Nana Gracilis' (above), *C. pisifera* 'Filifera Aurea' (below)

Conifer shoppers are blessed with a marvelous selection of false cypresses with varying colors, sizes, shapes and growth habits.

### Growing
False cypresses prefer **full sun**. The soil should be **fertile, moist, neutral to acidic** and **well drained**. Alkaline soils are tolerated. In shaded areas, growth may be sparse or thin.

### Tips
Tree varieties are used as specimen plants and for hedging and privacy screening. The dwarf and slow-growing cultivars are used in borders and rock gardens and as bonsai. False cypress shrubs can be grown near the house or as evergreen specimens in large containers.

### Recommended
Several species and many cultivars of false cypress are available. The scaley foliage comes in a drooping or strand form, in fan-like or feathery sprays and may be dark green, bright green or yellow. Plant forms vary too, from mounding or rounded to tall and pyramidal or narrow with pendulous branches. Check with your local garden center or nursery to see what is available. *C. obtusa* (Hinoki cypress) is a large, conical tree, but it has many popular cultivars that come in a wide range of sizes, including dwarf shrubs in the 1–6' range.

**Features:** narrow, pyramidal, evergreen tree or shrub, cultivars vary; foliage; habit; cones
**Height:** 1–150' **Spread:** 1–80'
**Hardiness:** zones 4–8

# Flowering Cherry, Plum & Almond

*Prunus*

P. subhirtella 'Pendula Rosea' (above)
P. x cistena (below)

A flowering cherry tree is so beautiful and uplifting after the gray days of winter that it can almost take your breath away.

## Growing

These flowering fruit trees prefer **full sun**. The soil should be of **average fertility, moist** and **well drained**. Shallow roots will emerge from the lawn if the tree is not getting sufficient water.

## Tips

*Prunus* species are beautiful as specimen plants and many are small enough to be included in almost any garden. Small species and cultivars can also be included in borders or grouped to form informal hedges or barriers. Pissard plum and purpleleaf sand cherry can be trained to form formal hedges.

Cherries can be rather short-lived. Choose pest and disease resistant species such as Sargent cherry or Higan cherry.

## Recommended

The following are a few popular selections. *P. cerasifera* '**Atropurpurea**' (Pissard plum) and *P.* x *cistena* (purpleleaf sand cherry) are shrubby plants grown for their purple foliage and light pink flowers. *P.* '**Hally Jolivette,**' a Long Island Gold Medal Award winner, is a rounded, bushy hybrid that has white double flowers with pink centers. It is cold hardy, grows relatively fast and can withstand stress. *P.* '**Kwanzan**' is a vase-shaped hybrid with gorgeous double pink flowers. *P. sargentii* (Sargent cherry), *P. serrulata* (Japanese flowering cherry) and *P. subhirtella* (Higan cherry) are rounded or spreading trees grown for their white or light pink flowers and their often attractive bark and bright fall color.

**Features:** upright, rounded, spreading or weeping, deciduous tree or shrub; spring to early-summer flowers; fruit; bark; fall foliage
**Height:** 4–75' **Spread:** 4–50'
**Hardiness:** zones 5–8

# Fothergilla
*Fothergilla*

*F. gardenii* 'Blue Mist' (above), *F. major* (below)

lowers, fragrance, fall color and interesting, soft tan to brownish stems give fothergillas year-round appeal.

## Growing
Fothergillas grow equally well in **full sun** or **partial shade**. In full sun these plants bear the most flowers and have the best fall color. The soil should be of **average fertility, acidic, humus rich, moist** and **well drained**.

## Tips
Fothergillas are attractive and useful in shrub or mixed borders, in woodland gardens and when combined with evergreen groundcover.

*The bottlebrush-shaped flowers of fothergillas have a delicate honey scent.*

## Recommended
*F. gardenii* (dwarf fothergilla) is a Long Island Gold Medal Award winner. The bushy shrub bears fragrant, white flowers. The foliage turns yellow, orange and red in fall. An added bonus is that it is relatively pest free.

*F. major* (large fothergilla) is a larger, rounded shrub that bears fragrant, white flowers. The fall colors are yellow, orange and scarlet.

Cultivars are available for both species.

**Features:** dense, rounded or bushy, deciduous shrub; fragrant, spring flowers; fall foliage
**Height:** 2–10'  **Spread:** 2–10'
**Hardiness:** zones 4–9

# Franklin Tree
*Franklinia*

This beautiful small tree offers lovely mid- to late-summer flowers and glorious, bright red or reddish purple fall color. Its gray bark is evident in winter.

## Growing

Franklin trees grow well in **full sun** or **partial shade,** with the best flower production and fall color occurring in full sun. The soil should be of **average fertility, humus rich, neutral to acidic, moist** and **well drained**.

## Tips

Franklin trees are small enough to be suitable in almost all gardens. In a smaller garden they can be used as shade trees, and in a larger garden they may be used as specimen trees or to provide light shade in a mixed or shrub border.

## Recommended

*F. alatamaha* is a small, upright tree with spreading branches that create an attractive, open appearance. It bears fragrant, white, cup-shaped flowers in mid- to late summer. The leaves turn bright red in fall.

*F. alatamaha* (above & below)

*This tree was discovered growing on the banks of the Altamaha river in Georgia by John Bertram in 1770. It is believed that there are no remaining wild specimens, because the tree was found in the wild on only two other documented occasions.*

**Also called:** Franklinia, Franklinia tree
**Features:** deciduous tree with an upright, open habit; late-summer flowers; fall color
**Height:** 10–20'  **Spread:** 6–15'
**Hardiness:** zones 5–8

# Golden Rain Tree

*Koelreuteria*

*K. paniculata* (above & below)

With its delicate clusters of yellow flowers and overall lacy appearance in summer, this lovely tree deserves wider use as a specimen or shade tree.

## Growing

Golden rain tree grows best in **full sun**. The soil should be **average to fertile, moist** and **well drained**. This fast-growing tree tolerates heat, drought, wind and polluted air. It also adapts to most alkaline or acidic soils.

## Tips

Golden rain tree makes an excellent shade or specimen tree for small properties. Its ability to adapt to a wide range of soils makes it useful in many garden situations. The fruit is not messy and will not stain patios or decks.

## Recommended

*K. paniculata* is an attractive, rounded, spreading tree. It bears long clusters of small, yellow flowers in mid-summer, followed by green capsular fruit with red tinges. The attractive leaves are somewhat lacy in appearance and may turn bright yellow in fall. Cultivars are available.

*This Asian species is one of the few trees with yellow flowers that bloom in mid- to late summer.*

**Features:** rounded, spreading, deciduous tree with attractive foliage, flowers and fruit
**Height:** 30–40' **Spread:** 30–40'
**Hardiness:** zones 5–8

# Hawthorn
*Crataegus*

*C. phaenopyrum* (above), *C. laevigata* (below)

The hawthorns are uncommonly beautiful trees, with a generous spring show of beautiful, apple-like blossoms, persistent, glossy red fruit and good fall color.

## Growing

Hawthorns grow equally well in **full sun** or **partial shade**. They adapt to any **well-drained soil** and tolerate urban conditions.

## Tips

Hawthorns can be grown as specimen plants or hedges in urban sites, lakeside gardens and exposed locations. They are popular in areas where vandalism is a problem because very few people wish to grapple with plants bearing stiff 2" long thorns. As a hedge, hawthorns create an almost impenetrable barrier.

These trees are small enough to include in most gardens. With the long, sharp thorns, however, a hawthorn might not be a good selection if there are children around.

## Recommended

*C. laevigata* (*C. oxyacantha;* English hawthorn) is a low-branching, rounded tree with zigzag layers of thorny branches. It bears white or pink flowers, followed by red fruit in late summer. Many cultivars are available.

*C. phaenopyrum* (*C. cordata;* Washington hawthorn) is an oval to rounded, thorny tree that bears white flowers and persistent, shiny red fruit in fall. The glossy green foliage turns red and orange in fall.

**Features:** rounded, deciduous tree, often with a zigzagged, layered branch pattern; late-spring or early-summer flowers; fruit; foliage; thorny branches **Height:** 15–35' **Spread:** 12–35' **Hardiness:** zones 3–8

# Holly
## *Ilex*

Hollies vary greatly in shape and size and have many attributes that stand out in the landscape.

### Growing

These plants prefer **full sun** but tolerate partial shade. The soil should be of **average to rich fertility, humus rich** and **moist**. Hollies perform best in **acidic soil** with a pH of 6.5 to 6 or lower. **Shelter** these plants from winter wind to help prevent the evergreen leaves from drying out and turning brown. Apply a summer mulch to keep the roots cool and moist.

### Tips

Hollies can be used in groups, in woodland gardens and in shrub and mixed borders; they can also be shaped into hedges. A holly tree also makes a great focal point in the landscape as a specimen plant. Winterberry is good for naturalizing in moist sites in the garden.

### Recommended

*I. glabra* (inkberry) is a rounded shrub with glossy, deep green, evergreen foliage and dark purple fruit. Cultivars are available. (Zones 4–9)

*I. x meserveae* (meserve holly, blue holly) is a group of hybrids developed from crosses between several hardy hollies and English holly (*I. aquifolium*). These dense, evergreen shrubs may be erect, mounding or spreading. (Zones 5–8)

*I. pedunculosa* (longstalk holly) is a Long Island Gold Medal Award winner.

*I.* x *meserveae* cultivar (above)
*I.* x *meserveae* 'Blue Girl' (below)

It is a bushy, upright, evergreen shrub or small tree with dark green glossy, spineless leaves and bright red fruit that can persist into early winter. (Zones 5–9)

*I. verticillata* (winterberry, winterberry holly) is a deciduous native species grown for its explosion of red fruit that persists into winter and constrasts with the snow. Many cultivars and hybrids are available. (Zones 3–9)

---

**Also called:** inkberry, winterberry
**Features:** erect or spreading, evergreen or deciduous shrub or tree; glossy, sometimes spiny foliage; fruit; habit **Height:** 3–50'
**Spread:** 3–40' **Hardiness:** zones 3–9

# Horsechestnut

*Aesculus*

A. parviflora (above), A. hippocastanum (below)

Horsechestnuts range from trees with immense regal bearing to small but impressive shrubs. All have spectacular flowers.

## Growing

Horsechestnuts grow well in **full sun** or **partial shade**. The soil should be **fertile**, **moist** and **well drained**. These trees dislike excessive drought.

## Tips

Horsechestnuts are used as specimen and shade trees. The roots of horsechestnuts can break up sidewalks and patios if planted too close. The smaller, shrubby horsechestnuts grow well near pond plantings and also make interesting specimens. Give them plenty of space as they can form large colonies.

## Recommended

*A. hippocastanum* (common horsechestnut) is a large, rounded tree that branches right to the ground if grown in an open setting. The flowers, white with yellow or pink marks, are borne in long spikes. (Zones 3–7)

*A. parviflora* (bottlebrush buckeye) is a spreading, mound-forming, suckering shrub that has plentiful spikes of creamy white flowers. (Zones 4–9)

*A. pavia* (red buckeye) is a low-growing to rounded shrubby tree with lovely foliage and cherry red flowers that will stop you in your tracks. It needs consistent moisture. (Zones 4–8)

*These trees give heavy shade, which is excellent for cooling buildings but makes it difficult to grow grass beneath the trees.*

**Also called:** buckeye **Features:** rounded or spreading, deciduous tree or shrub; early-summer flowers; foliage; spiny fruit **Height:** 8–80' **Spread:** 8–65' **Hardiness:** zones 3–9

# Hydrangea

*Hydrangea*

Hydrangeas have many attractive qualities including showy, often long-lasting flowers and glossy green leaves, some of which turn beautiful colors in fall.

## Growing

Hydrangeas grow well in **full sun** or **partial shade,** and some species tolerate full shade. Shade or partial shade will reduce leaf and flower scorch in hotter gardens. The soil should be of **average to high fertility, humus rich, moist** and **well drained**. These plants perform best in cool, moist conditions.

## Tips

Hydrangeas come in many forms and have many uses in the landscape. They can be included in shrub or mixed borders, used as specimens or informal barriers and planted in groups or containers.

## Recommended

*H. arborescens* (smooth hydrangea) is a rounded shrub that flowers well even in shady conditions. This species is rarely grown in favor of the cultivars that bear large clusters of showy white blossoms. (Zones 3–9)

*H. macrophylla* (bigleaf hydrangea) is a rounded shrub that bears flowers in shades of pink, red, blue or purple from mid- to late summer. Many cultivars are available. (Zones 5–9)

*H. paniculata* (panicle hydrangea) is a spreading to upright, large shrub or small tree that bears white flowers from late summer to early fall. **'Grandiflora'**

*H. querquifolia* (above)
*H. macrophylla* cultivar (below)

(Peegee hydrangea) is a commonly available cultivar. (Zones 4–8)

*H. quercifolia* (oakleaf hydrangea) is a Long Island Gold Medal Award winner. It is a mound-forming shrub with attractive, cinnamon brown, exfoliating bark and large leaves that are lobed like an oak's and turn bronze to bright red in fall. It also has conical clusters of sterile and fertile flowers. (Zones 4–8)

**Features:** deciduous; mounding or spreading shrub or tree; flowers; habit; foliage; bark
**Height:** 3–20' **Spread:** 3–10'
**Hardiness:** zones 3–9

# Juniper
*Juniperus*

*J. horizontalis* 'Blue Chip' (above), *J. horizontalis* 'Blue Prince' (below)

There may be a juniper in every gardener's future. The many choices available range from low, creeping plants to upright, pyramidal forms.

## Growing

Junipers prefer **full sun** but tolerate light shade. Ideally the soil should be of **average fertility** and **well drained,** but these plants tolerate most conditions.

## Tips

With the wide variety of junipers available, there are endless uses for them in the garden. They make prickly barriers and hedges, and they can be used in borders, as specimens or in groups. The larger species can be used to form windbreaks, while the low-growing species can be used in rock gardens and as groundcover.

## Recommended

Junipers vary, not just from species to species, but often within a species. Cultivars are available for all species and may differ significantly from the species. **J. chinensis** (Chinese juniper) is a conical tree or spreading shrub. **J. horizontalis** (creeping juniper) is a prostrate, creeping groundcover. **J. procumbens** (Japanese garden juniper) is a wide-spreading, stiff-branched, low shrub. **J. scopulorum** (Rocky Mountain juniper) can be upright, rounded, weeping or spreading. **J. squamata** (singleseed juniper) forms a prostrate or low, spreading shrub or a small, upright tree. **J. virginiana** (eastern redcedar) is a durable tree that can be upright or wide-spreading.

**Features:** conical or columnar tree, rounded or spreading shrub, prostrate groundcover; evergreen; foliage; variety of colors, sizes and habits  **Height:** 4"–80'  **Spread:** 18"–25'
**Hardiness:** zones 3–9

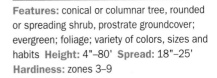

# Katsura-Tree
*Cercidiphyllum*

Katsura-tree adds distinction and grace to the garden at any stage of its growth. Even in youth it is poised and elegant, and as a mature tree it is a bewitching specimen.

### Growing
Katsura-tree grows equally well in **full sun** or **partial shade**. The soil should be **fertile, humus rich, neutral to acidic, moist** and **well drained**. In order to become established, a newly planted tree must be watered regularly during dry spells for the first two years after it is planted.

### Tips
Katsura-tree is useful as a specimen or shade tree. The species is quite large and is best used in large gardens, whereas the cultivar 'Pendula,' although it spreads quite wide, can be used in smaller gardens.

### Recommended
*C. japonicum* is a slow-growing tree with heart-shaped, blue-green leaves that turn yellow and orange in fall and develop a spicy fragrance. **'Pendula'** is one of the most elegant weeping trees available. It is usually grafted to a standard, and the mounding, cascading branches give the entire tree the appearance of a waterfall tumbling over rocks.

*C. japonicum* 'Pendula' (above)
*C. japonicum* (below)

*Katsura-tree is native to eastern Asia, and its delicate foliage blends well into Japanese-style gardens.*

---

**Features:** rounded, spreading or weeping, often multi-stemmed, deciduous tree with attractive summer and fall foliage
**Height:** 10–65' **Spread:** 10–65'
**Hardiness:** zones 4–8

# Lilac
*Syringa*

S. meyeri (above), S. vulgaris (below)

The blooming of lilac trees is a sure sign that spring is here to stay. With hundreds of cultivars, lilacs offer color, fragrance and lovely spring ambiance to the garden.

## Growing
Lilacs grow best in **full sun**. The soil should be **fertile, humus rich** and **well drained**. These plants tolerate open, windy locations.

## Tips
Include lilacs in a shrub or mixed border or use them to create an informal hedge. They can also offer summer privacy screening. Japanese tree lilac can be used as a specimen tree.

## Recommended
**S. x *hyacinthiflora*** (hyacinth-flowered lilac, early-flowering lilac) is a group of hardy, upright hybrids that become spreading as they mature. Clusters of fragrant flowers appear two weeks earlier than those of the French lilacs. The leaves turn reddish purple in fall. Many cultivars are available. (Zones 3–7)

**S. *meyeri*** (Meyer lilac) is a compact, rounded shrub that bears fragrant, pink or lavender flowers. (Zones 3–7)

**S. *reticulata*** (Japanese tree lilac) is a large, rounded shrub or small tree that bears white flowers. 'Ivory Silk' has a more compact habit and produces more flowers than the species. This fragrant tree has few pest problems. (Zones 3–7)

**S. *vulgaris*** (French lilac, common lilac) is the plant that comes to mind for most people when they think of lilacs. It is a suckering, spreading shrub with an irregular habit. It bears fragrant, lilac-colored flowers. Hundreds of cultivars with a variety of flower colors are available. (Zones 3–8)

**Features:** rounded or suckering, deciduous shrub or small tree; late-spring to mid-summer flowers; habit **Height:** 3–30' **Spread:** 3–25' **Hardiness:** zones 2–8

# Linden

*Tilia*

*L*indens are picturesque shade trees with a signature gumdrop shape and sweet-scented flowers that capture the essence of summer.

## Growing

Lindens grow best in **full sun**. The soil should be **average to fertile, moist** and **well drained**. These trees adapt to most pH levels but prefer an **alkaline soil**. They tolerate pollution and urban conditions.

## Tips

Lindens are useful and attractive street trees, shade trees and specimen trees. Their tolerance of pollution and their moderate size make lindens ideal for city gardens.

## Recommended

*T. cordata* (littleleaf linden) is a dense, pyramidal tree that may become rounded with age. It bears small, fragrant flowers with narrow, yellow-green bracts. Cultivars are available.

*T. tomentosa* (silver linden) has a broad, pyramidal or rounded habit and bears small, fragrant flowers. It has glossy green leaves with fuzzy, silvery undersides.

*T. cordata* (above)

*Given enough space to spread, lindens will branch right to the ground.*

**Features:** dense, pyramidal to rounded, deciduous tree; habit; foliage **Height:** 20–65' **Spread:** 15–50' **Hardiness:** zones 3–8

# Magnolia
*Magnolia*

*[handwritten: no deciduous 20fw. 40-50 259 Dollars.]*

M. stellata (above), M. x soulangeana (below)

*Many hybrid magnolias have been introduced in recent years, including hardier, later-flowering selections and yellow-flowered selections.*

*[handwritten: Camelia $129 and not deciduous]*

Magnolias are beautiful, fragrant, versatile plants that also provide attractive winter structure.

### Growing
Magnolias grow well in **full sun** or **partial shade**. The soil should be **fertile, humus rich, acidic, moist** and **well drained**. A summer mulch will help keep the roots cool and the soil moist.

### Tips
Magnolias are used as specimen trees, and the smaller species can be used in borders. Avoid planting magnolias where the morning sun will encourage the blooms to open too early in the season. A spring frost will damage the blossoms but not permanently: they will be back next year.

### Recommended
Many species, hybrids and cultivars, in a range of sizes and with differing flowering times and flower colors, are available. Two of the most common are **M. x *soulangeana*** (saucer magnolia), a rounded, spreading, deciduous shrub or tree with eye-catching pink, purple or white flowers; and **M. *stellata*** (star magnolia), a lovely compact, bushy or spreading, deciduous shrub or small tree with many-petalled, fragrant, white flowers. Check with your local nursery or garden center for other available magnolias.

**Features:** upright to spreading, deciduous shrub or tree; flowers; fruit; foliage; habit; bark
**Height:** 8–40' **Spread:** 5–35'
**Hardiness:** zones 3–9

# Maple
*Acer*

*A. palmatum* cultivar (above), *A. griseum* (below)

Maples are attractive year-round, with delicate flowers in spring, attractive foliage and hanging samaras in summer, vibrant leaf color in fall and interesting bark and branch structures in winter. They are some of the most popular shade trees.

## Growing

Generally, maples do well in **full sun** or **light shade,** but some species favor different light levels. The soil should be **fertile, moist, high in organic matter** and **well drained.**

## Tips

Maples can be used as specimen trees, as large elements in shrub or mixed borders or as hedges. Some maples are useful as understory plants bordering wooded areas; others can be grown in containers on patios or terraces. Few Japanese gardens are without the attractive smaller maples. Almost all maples can be used to create bonsai specimens.

## Recommended

Many maples are very large when fully mature, but there are also a few smaller species, including **A. campestre** (hedge maple), **A. ginnala** (amur maple), **A. griseum** (paperbark maple), **A. palmatum** (Japanese maple) and **A. rubrum** (red maple). Check with your local nursery or garden center for availability.

**Features:** small, multi-stemmed, deciduous tree or large shrub; foliage; bark; winged fruit; fall color; form; flowers **Height:** 6–80' **Spread:** 6–70' **Hardiness:** zones 2–8

# Mountain Ash
*Sorbus*

S. *alnifolia* (both photos)

The mountain ash adds beauty to the garden in all four seasons. It flowers in spring, its attractive summer foliage turns brilliant colors in fall and it has persistent fruit that adds color to the tree's attractive form in winter.

## Growing
Mountain ash grows well in **full sun** or **light shade**. The soil should be of **average fertility, humus rich** and

*The leaves of Korean mountain ash have a shape distinct from those of other mountain ash species—its leaves resemble beech leaves rather than consisting of the usual narrow leaflets along a central stem.*

**well drained**. Mountain ash adapts to a wide range of pH levels but does not tolerate pollution.

## Tips
Mountain ash makes a lovely specimen in a medium-sized or larger garden. Avoid planting it near busy streets and in urban areas where pollution can be a problem.

## Recommended
*S. alnifolia* (Korean mountain ash) is a Long Island Gold Medal Award winner. It is a rounded to conical tree that produces dense clusters of small, white flowers in spring, followed by pink, red or scarlet fruit in fall. The bright green foliage turns yellow, orange, red or golden brown in fall.

**Features:** rounded or conical, deciduous tree with attractive flowers, foliage, fruit, bark and habit **Height:** 40–60' **Spread:** 20–40' **Hardiness:** zones 4–7

# Oak

*Quercus*

Q. *robur* (above & below)

The mighty oak's classic shape, stateliness, outstanding fall color, deep roots and long life are some of its many assets. Plant it for its individual beauty and shade value.

## Growing

Oaks grow well in **full sun** or **partial shade**. The soil should be **fertile, moist** and **well drained**. These trees can be difficult to establish; transplant them only while they are young.

## Tips

Oaks are large trees that are best as specimens or for groves in parks and large gardens. Do not disturb the ground around the base of an oak; this tree is very sensitive to changes in grade.

## Recommended

Among the many oaks to choose from, there are a few popular species. *Q. alba* (white oak) is a rounded, spreading tree with peeling bark and purple-red fall color. *Q. coccinea* (scarlet oak) is noted for having the most brilliant red fall color of all the oaks. *Q. robur* (English oak) is a rounded, spreading tree with golden yellow fall color. *Q. rubra* (red oak) is a rounded, spreading tree with fall color ranging from yellow to red-brown. Some cultivars are available; check with your local nursery or garden center.

**Features:** large, rounded, spreading, deciduous tree; summer and fall foliage; bark; habit; acorns **Height:** 35–120' **Spread:** 10–100' **Hardiness:** zones 3–9

# Pine

*Pinus*

Pines offer exciting possibilities for any garden. Their evergreen nature offers year-round foliage with bold to fine textures.

## Growing

Pines grow best in **full sun**. These trees adapt to most **well-drained soils** but do not tolerate polluted urban conditions.

## Tips

Pines can be used as specimen trees, hedges, windbreaks and for privacy screens. Smaller cultivars can be included in shrub or mixed borders and rock gardens. These trees are not heavy feeders; fertilizing will encourage rapid new growth that is weak and susceptible to pest and disease problems.

## Recommended

There are many available pines, both as trees and as shrubby dwarf plants. Check with your local garden center or nursery to see what is available.

*P. strobus* 'Contorta' (above), *P. strobus* (below)

*When buying pine trees for your landscape, select varieties that are disease resistant.*

**Features:** upright, columnar or spreading, evergreen tree; foliage; bark; cones; habit
**Height:** 2–120' **Spread:** 2–60'
**Hardiness:** zones 2–8

# Plum Yew

*Cephalotaxus*

*C. harringtonia* 'Duke Gardens' (above & below)

Plum yew gives gardeners an excellent choice for shaded areas of the garden, and it is one of the very few evergreens that thrive in shaded conditions.

## Growing

Plum yew grows best in **light or partial shade**, but it tolerates full shade and full sun. The soil should be **fertile, moist** and **well drained**.

## Tips

Plum yew can be grown as a specimen or in groups, and it can be included in woodland gardens, mass plantings and shaded borders. It is a good replacement for junipers and yews.

## Recommended

*C. harringtonia* is a spreading evergreen shrub or small tree with glossy dark green needles. It produces clusters of small, green, oval fruits that ripen to purple-brown in fall. **'Duke Gardens'** is a Long Island Gold Medal Award winner. It is a popular dwarf form with very dark green (almost black) needles. It is more tolerant of full sun than the species and is more cold hardy, but it does need protection from the wind. Once established, it is relatively drought tolerant. It grows about 3' tall and spreads about 4'. Other cultivars are also available.

**Features:** spreading evergreen shrub or small tree with attractive foliage and fruit
**Height:** 3–30' **Spread:** 3–30'
**Hardiness:** zones 5–9

# Redbud
*Cercis*

Redbud is an outstanding treasure of spring. Deep magenta flowers bloom before the leaves emerge, and their impact is intense. As the buds open, the flowers turn pink, covering the long, thin branches in pastel clouds.

## Growing

Redbud will grow well in **full sun, partial shade** or **light shade**. The soil should be a **fertile, deep loam** that is **moist** and **well drained**. This plant has tender roots and does not like being transplanted.

## Tips

Redbud can be used as a specimen tree, in a shrub or mixed border or in a woodland garden. Avoid planting trees where they will be stressed, because stressed trees tend to be susceptible to diseases.

## Recommended

*C. canadensis* (eastern redbud) is a spreading, multi-stemmed tree that bears red, purple or pink flowers. The young foliage is bronze, fading to green over the summer and turning bright yellow in fall. Many beautiful cultivars are available.

*C. canadensis* (above & below)

*Redbud is not as long-lived as many other trees, so use its delicate beauty to supplement more permanent trees in the garden.*

**Features:** rounded or spreading, multi-stemmed, deciduous tree or shrub; spring flowers; fall foliage **Height:** 20–30' **Spread:** 25–35' **Hardiness:** zones 4–9

# Rhododendron

*Rhododendron*

R. 'Purple Gem' (above), Azalea hybrid (below)

*E*ven when not covered in a stunning display of brightly colored flowers, rhododendrons are wonderful landscape plants.

## Growing

Rhododendrons and evergreen azaleas grow best in **partial shade** or **light shade,** while the deciduous azaleas typically grow best in **full sun** or **partial shade**. Choose a location that is **sheltered** from drying winter winds. The soil should be **fertile, humus rich, acidic, moist** and **well drained**. A good mulch is important to keep the soil moist and to protect the shallow roots of these plants.

## Tips

Rhododendrons and azaleas perform best and look most attractive when planted in groups. Use them in shrub or mixed borders, in woodland gardens and in sheltered rock gardens.

## Recommended

These bushy shrubs vary greatly in size and hardiness, may be evergreen or deciduous and bear flowers in a huge range of colors. There are hundreds of rhododendron and azalea species, hybrids and cultivars available. Visit your local garden center or specialty grower to see what is available.

---

**Also called:** azalea **Features:** upright, mounding, rounded, evergreen or deciduous shrub; late-winter to early-summer flowers; foliage; habit **Height:** 2–12' **Spread:** 2–12' **Hardiness:** zones 3–8

# Rose-of-Sharon

*Hibiscus*

*H. syriacus* 'Diana' (above), *H. syriacus* 'Red Heart' (below)

Rose-of-Sharon is one of a few flowering trees or shrubs that offers color in the summer garden.

## Growing

Rose-of-Sharon prefers **full sun** and tolerates partial shade with fewer flowers and leggier growth. The soil should be of **average fertility, humus rich, moist** and **well drained**. Pinch plants back when young to encourage bushy growth. Rose-of-Sharon can tolerate periods of drought.

## Tips

Rose-of-Sharon is best used in shrub or mixed borders. It can also be used to create a focal point or you can train it into a tree form for a small garden.

## Recommended

*H. syriacus* is an erect, multi-stemmed shrub that bears dark pink flowers from mid-summer to fall. There are many cultivars with flowers in a wide range of shades of pink and purple as well as white. A popular cultivar is **'Diana,'** with gracious, large, pure white, ruffled flowers. It is very drought tolerant.

**Also called:** hibiscus, hardy hibiscus
**Features:** summer to fall flowers in shades of pink, purple and white  **Height:** 8–12'
**Spread:** 6–10'  **Hardiness:** zones 5–9

# Russian Arborvitae
## *Microbiota*

*M. decussata* (above & below)

This tree is one of the most beautiful of the low, groundcovering evergreens. Its delicate, green shoots develop an interesting purple tinge in winter.

## Growing

Russian arborvitae grows well in **full sun** or **partial shade**. The soil should be **fertile, moist** and **well drained**. These tough plants are able to survive cold weather, but they suffer in more pleasant climates. Hot weather and heavy soil will stress the plant and may shorten its life considerably. Root rot can occur in poorly drained soils.

## Tips

This attractive plant makes a great addition to shrub borders, and it is enough of a low grower to be used as a groundcover. It can be used to fill in unused corners of the garden and will help prevent erosion on slopes too steep for mowing. A few plants will spread to fill a fairly large area.

## Recommended

*M. descussata* is a Long Island Gold Medal Award winner. It is a low-growing, spreading, bushy, evergreen groundcover that grows to a height of 12–18" and spreads about 8–12" per year. The leaves are scale-like and give the shoots an attractive, delicate, stringy or thread-like appearance. The leaves turn purple-brown in fall.

**Features:** mound-forming, spreading, evergreen shrub; attractive shoots and foliage
**Height:** 12–18" **Spread:** 3' or more
**Hardiness:** zones 3–7

# Serviceberry
*Amelanchier*

A. canadensis (above), A. arborea (below)

*Serviceberry fruit can be used in place of blueberries in any recipe—they have a similar but generally sweeter flavor.*

The *Amelanchier* species are first-rate North American natives, bearing lacy, white flowers in spring, followed by edible berries in summer. In fall, the foliage color ranges from a glowing apricot to a deep red.

### Growing

Serviceberries grow well in **full sun** or **light shade**. They prefer **acidic soil** that is **fertile, humus rich, moist** and **well drained**. They adjust to drought conditions.

### Tips

With spring flowers, edible fruit, attractive leaves that turn red in fall and often artistic branch growth, serviceberries make beautiful specimen plants or even shade trees in small gardens. The shrubbier forms can be grown along the edges of a woodland or in a border. In the wild, these trees are often found growing near water sources, and they are beautiful beside ponds or streams.

### Recommended

Several popular species and hybrids are available. *A. arborea* (downy serviceberry, Juneberry, shadbush) is a small, single- or multi-stemmed tree. *A. canadensis* (shadblow serviceberry) is a large, upright, suckering shrub. *A. x grandiflora* (apple serviceberry) is a small, spreading, often multi-stemmed tree. All three forms have white flowers, purple fruit and great fall color.

---

**Also called:** saskatoon, juneberry
**Features:** single- or multi-stemmed, deciduous, large shrub or small tree; spring or early-summer flowers; edible fruit; fall color; habit; bark **Height:** 4–30' **Spread:** 4–30'
**Hardiness:** zones 3–9

# Snowbell
*Styrax*

S. obassia (both photos)

Snowbells are easy to admire for their delicate, shapely appearance and the dangling flowers that are clustered along the undersides of the branches.

## Growing
Snowbells grow well in **full sun, partial shade** or **light shade**. The soil should be **fertile, humus rich, neutral to acidic, moist** and **well drained**.

*Plant a snowbell next to your patio so you can admire the flowers from below as you stretch out in a lounge chair.*

## Tips
Snowbells can be used to provide light shade in shrub or mixed borders. They can also be included in woodland gardens, and they make interesting specimens near entryways or patios.

## Recommended
**S. obassia** (fragrant snowbell) is a broad, columnar tree that bears white flowers in long clusters at the branch ends in early summer.

**Features:** upright, rounded, spreading or columnar, deciduous tree; late-spring to early-summer flowers; foliage; habit
**Height:** 20–40' **Spread:** 20–30'
**Hardiness:** zones 4–8

# Spirea

*Spiraea*

*S. japonica* 'Little Princess' (above), *S. x vanhouttei* (below)

Spireas, seen in so many gardens and with dozens of cultivars, remain undeniable favorites. With a wide range of forms, sizes and colors of both foliage and flowers, spireas have many possible uses in the landscape.

## Growing

Spireas prefer **full sun** The soil should be **fertile, acidic, moist** and **well drained**.

## Tips

Spireas are used in shrub or mixed borders, in rock gardens and as informal screens and hedges.

## Recommended

Many species and cultivars of spireas are available. The following are a few popular hybrid groups.

***S. japonica*** (*S. x bumalda*) is a low, broad, mounded shrub with pink flowers. It is rarely grown in favor of the many cultivars, which also have pink flowers but often with brightly colored foliage.

***S. prunifolia*** (bridalwreath spirea) produces double white flowers on arching branches.

***S. thunbergii*** (thunberg spirea) is a dense, bushy shrub with arching stems, light green foliage and white, spring to early-summer flowers.

***S. x vanhouttei*** (Vanhoutte spirea) is a dense, bushy shrub with arching branches that bear clusters of white flowers. Check your local nursery or garden center to see what cultivars and hybrids are available.

**Features:** round, bushy, deciduous shrub; summer flowers; habit **Height:** 1–10' **Spread:** 1–12' **Hardiness:** zones 3–9

# Spruce
*Picea*

The spruce is one of the most commonly grown and most commonly abused evergreens. To enjoy a spruce tree in all its potential glory, grow it where it has enough room to spread, then let it branch all the way to the ground.

### Growing

Spruce trees grow best in **full sun**. The soil should be **deep, moist, well drained** and **neutral to acidic**. These trees generally don't like hot, dry or polluted conditions. Spruces are best grown from small, young stock because they dislike being transplanted when they are larger or more mature.

### Tips

Spruces are generally used as specimen trees. The dwarf and slow-growing cultivars can also be used in shrub or mixed borders. These trees look most attractive when they are allowed to keep their lower branches.

### Recommended

Spruces are generally upright, pyramidal trees, but cultivars may be low-growing, wide-spreading or even weeping in habit. Popular and commonly available species include *P. abies* (Norway spruce); *P. glauca* (white spruce); *P. omorika* (Serbian spruce); *P. orientalis* (Oriental spruce), a Long Island Gold Medal Award winner; *P. pungens* (Colorado spruce); and their cultivars.

*P. glauca* 'Conica' (above)
*P. pungens* var. *glauca* 'Moerheim' (below)

*Oil-based pesticides such as dormant oil can take the blue out of your blue-needled spruces. Growth that fills in after the application of these pesticides will still have the blue color.*

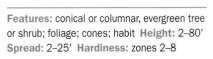

**Features:** conical or columnar, evergreen tree or shrub; foliage; cones; habit **Height:** 2–80'
**Spread:** 2–25' **Hardiness:** zones 2–8

# St. Johnswort
*Hypericum*

*H. frondosum* (above)
*H. frondosum* 'Sunburst' (right)

Masses of bright yellow flowers with numerous, showy, hair-like stamens add sunshine to the summer garden.

## Growing

St. Johnswort grows best in **full sun** but will tolerate partial shade. The soil should be of **average fertility** and **well drained,** though this plant adapts to most soils as long as they aren't too wet. It tolerates drought and heavy, rocky or very alkaline soils.

*Many medicinal and magical properties have been attributed to St. Johnswort species.*

## Tips

St. Johnswort makes a wonderful addition to a mixed or shrub border, where the late-summer flowers can brighten up a planting that is looking tired or faded in the heat of summer. This durable shrub is also useful for difficult areas where the soil is poor and watering is difficult or too costly.

## Recommended

*H. frondosum* forms a rounded, upright mound. This deciduous species grows 2–4' tall, with an equal spread. Bright yellow flowers are borne in mid- and late summer. The long, dense stamens give each flower a fuzzy appearance. **'Sunburst'** is a Long Island Gold Medal Award winner. It bears larger flowers than the species and has exfoliating, red-brown bark.

---

**Also called:** golden St. Johnswort
**Features:** rounded, mounding, deciduous shrub; summer to fall flowers; attractive foliage
**Height:** 2–4'  **Spread:** 2–4'
**Hardiness:** zones 5–8

# Stephanandra

*Stephanandra*

Stephanandra is a tough, disease-free plant that has a vigorous growing habit, making it a lovely specimen plant. It can also be shaped into a dwarf hedge.

## Growing

Stephanandra grows well in **full sun, light shade** or **partial shade**. The soil should be **fertile, humus rich, moist** and **well drained**.

## Tips

Stephanandra can be put to a variety of uses. Include it in a shrub border or in an informal hedge, or mass plant it to create a screen or prevent soil erosion.

## Recommended

*S. incisa* forms a dense thicket of attractive arching shoots. The sharply lobed leaves turn shades of yellow and orange in fall. It bears inconspicuous clusters of small, creamy white flowers in summer, and it grows 4–6' tall with an equal spread. **'Crispa'** is a Long Island Gold Medal Award winner. It is a dwarf cultivar that is actually grown more often than the species. In fall, the foliage turns lovely shades of apricot, maroon and purple. The deeply lobed leaves have wavy margins and the branches are self-rooting. This cultivar grows 2–3' tall with an equal spread.

*S. incisa* (above)

*This fast-growing shrub suckers freely, making it a useful choice when you want to fill in a large area quickly. You may also want to avoid planting stephanandra next to less vigorous plants because it will quickly outcompete such companions.*

---

**Also called:** cut-leaf stephanandra
**Features:** thicket-forming, deciduous shrub; attractive foliage and bark; fall color
**Height:** 2–6'  **Spread:** 2–6'
**Hardiness:** zones 3–7

# Stewartia
*Stewartia*

S. pseudocamellia (above)

*Don't be concerned if the bark doesn't put on a display when you first plant your stewartia. It takes several years for the tree to mature enough for the flaking to develop.*

This lovely tree adds beauty to your garden all year long, with dark green summer foliage, summer flowers, colorful fall foliage and exfoliating bark.

### Growing
Stewartia grows well in **full sun** or **light shade**. The soil should be of **average to high fertility, humus rich, neutral to acidic, moist** and **well drained**. Provide **shelter** from strong winds. Transplant these trees when they are very young as the roots resent being disturbed.

### Tips
Stewartia is used as a specimen tree and in group plantings. It makes a great companion for rhododendrons and azaleas because it provides the light shade they enjoy, and all these plants grow well in similar soil conditions.

### Recommended
*S. pseudocamellia* (Japanese stewartia) is a Long Island Gold Medal Award winner. It is a broad, columnar or pyramidal tree. White flowers with showy yellow stamens appear in mid-summer. The dark green leaves turn shades of yellow, orange, scarlet and reddish purple in fall. The bark is scaly and exfoliating, leaving the trunk mottled with gray, orange, pink and reddish brown. Cultivars are available.

**Features:** broad, conical or rounded, deciduous tree; mid-summer flowers; summer and fall foliage; exfoliating bark **Height:** 20–35' **Spread:** 20–35' **Hardiness:** zones 5–7

# Summersweet Clethra

*Clethra*

Summersweet clethra is one of the best shrubs for adding fragrance to your garden. It also attracts butterflies and other pollinators.

## Growing

Summersweet clethra grows best in **full to partial sun, light shade** or **full shade**. The soil should be **fertile, humus rich, acidic, moist** and **well drained**.

## Tips

Although not aggressive, this shrub tends to sucker, forming a colony of stems. Use it in a border or in a woodland garden. The light shade along the edge of a woodland garden is also an ideal location.

## Recommended

***C. alnifolia* var. *compacta*** is a Long Island Gold Medal Award winner. It is a large, rounded, upright, colony-forming shrub. It grows 3–8' tall, spreading 3–6' and bears attractive spikes of white flowers in mid- to late summer. The foliage turns yellow in fall. Several cultivars are available, including pink-flowered selections.

*C. alnifolia* var. *compacta* (above & below)

*Summersweet clethra is useful in damp, shaded gardens, where the late-season flowers are much appreciated.*

---

**Also called:** sweet pepperbush
**Features:** rounded, suckering deciduous shrub; fragrant summer flowers; attractive habit; colorful fall foliage **Height:** 2–8'
**Spread:** 3–8' **Hardiness:** zones 3–9

# Sweetbox
*Sarcococca*

S. hookeriana var. humilis (above & below)

Sweetbox's dark green evergreen foliage and shade tolerance makes it an excellent woodland plant.

## Growing

Sweetbox grows best in **full, light or partial shade,** but it tolerates full sun if kept consistently moist. The soil should be **average to fertile, humus rich, moist** and **well drained**.

## Tips

Sweetbox is a useful plant for creating hedges in shaded situations. Its dark green glossy foliage makes a great background plant for the more brightly colored flowers of other plants in herbaceous and mixed borders. Var. *humilis* also makes a good groundcover under trees and in other shaded sites.

## Recommended

*S. hookeriana* forms a dense, mounding thicket of stems. It spreads by suckers (but not aggressively) to form drifts. It bears fragrant, white flowers from late winter to early spring, sometimes followed by shiny black fruit that persists into winter. It grows 4–6' tall with an equal or greater spread. **Var. *humilis*** is a Long Island Gold Medal Award winner. It is a dwarf form that is far more commonly available than the species. It grows 12–24" tall and spreads about 36". It is relatively drought tolerant and pest free. Avoid overhead watering. It is also hardier than the species, thriving in zone 5–8 gardens.

---

**Features:** thicket-forming evergreen shrub; glossy dark green foliage; fragrant, white, late-winter to spring flowers **Height:** 1–6' **Spread:** 3–6' or more **Hardiness:** zones 6–8

# Viburnum

*Viburnum*

Excellent fall color, beautiful form, shade tolerance, scented flowers and attractive fruit put the viburnums in a class by themselves.

## Growing

Viburnums grow well in **full sun, partial shade** or **light shade**. The soil should be of **average fertility, moist** and **well drained**. Viburnums tolerate both **alkaline and acidic soils**.

These plants will look neatest if dead-headed, but this practice prevents fruit from forming. Fruiting is more prolific when more than one plant of a species is grown.

## Tips

Viburnums can be used in borders and woodland gardens. They are a great choice for plantings near swimming pools.

## Recommended

Many popular viburnum species, hybrids and cultivars are available. *V. carlesii* (Korean spice viburnum) is a dense, bushy, rounded, deciduous shrub with white or pink, spicy-scented flowers (zones 5–8). *V. dilatatum* **'Erie'** (linden viburnum) is a Long Island Gold Medal Award winner that is a large, mound-forming, deciduous shrub with large clusters of creamy spring flowers, persistent, bright red or orange fruit and yellow fall foliage (zones 4–7). *V. opulus* (European cranberrybush) is a rounded, spreading, deciduous shrub with lacy-looking flower clusters (zones

*V. opulus* (above), *V. plicatum* var. *tomentosum* (below)

3–8). *V. plicatum* **var. *tomentosum*** (doublefile viburnum) has lacy-looking, white flower clusters and a graceful, horizontal branching pattern that gives the shrub a layered effect (zones 5–8). *V. trilobum* (American cranberrybush) is a dense, rounded shrub with clusters of white flowers followed by red fruit (zones 2–7).

---

**Features:** bushy or spreading, evergreen, semi-evergreen or deciduous shrub; flowers (some fragrant); summer and fall foliage; fruit; habit **Height:** 18"–20' **Spread:** 18"–15' **Hardiness:** zones 2–8

# Weigela
*Weigela*

Weigelas have been improved through breeding, and specimens with more compact forms, longer flowering periods and greater cold tolerance are now available.

## Growing
Weigelas prefer **full sun** but tolerate partial shade. The soil should be **fertile** and **well drained**. These plants will adapt to most well-drained soil conditions.

## Tips
Weigelas can be used in shrub or mixed borders, in open woodland gardens and as informal barrier plantings.

## Recommended
*W. florida* is a spreading shrub with arching branches that bear clusters of dark pink flowers. Many hybrids and cultivars are available, including dwarf varieties, red-, pink- or white-flowered varieties and varieties with purple, bronze or yellow foliage

*W. florida* 'Variegata' (above), *W. florida* (below)

*Weigela is one of the longest-blooming shrubs, with the main flush of blooms lasting as long as six weeks. It often re-blooms if sheared lightly after the first flowers fade.*

**Features:** upright or low, spreading, deciduous shrub; late-spring to early-summer flowers; foliage; habit **Height:** 1–9' **Spread:** 1–12' **Hardiness:** zones 3–8

# Willow
*Salix*

These fast-growing deciduous shrubs or trees can have colorful or twisted stems or foliage, and they come in a huge range of growth habits and sizes.

## Growing
Willows grow best in **full sun.** The soil should be of **average fertility, moist** and **well drained,** though some of the shrubby species are drought resistant.

## Tips
Reserve large tree willows for big spaces—they look particularly attractive near water features. Smaller willows can be used as small specimen trees or in shrub and mixed borders. Include small and trailing forms in rock gardens and along retaining walls.

S. *alba* 'Tristis' (above)

## Recommended
The following are just a few of the many popular willows available.

**S. *alba* 'Tristis'** is a deciduous, rounded tree with delicate, flexible, weeping branches that sweep the ground. The young growth and fall leaves are bright yellow. (Zones 4–8)

**S. *integra* 'Hakuro Nishiki'** (dappled willow, Japanese dappled willow) is a lovely spreading shrub or small tree with supple, arching branches that appear almost weeping. The young shoots are orange-pink in color and the leaves are dappled green, cream and pink. (Zones 5–8)

---

**Features:** bushy or arching shrub, or spreading or weeping tree; summer and fall foliage; stems; habit **Height:** 1–65' **Spread:** 3–65' **Hardiness:** zones 3–8

# Winter Hazel

*Corylopsis*

*C. pauciflora* (both photos)

Plants that flower as winter is barely over are perhaps the most welcome of all—they assure us that warmer weather is on its way.

### Growing

Winter hazel grows well in **full sun, partial shade or light shade**. The soil should be **fertile, humus rich, moist** and **well drained**. The growing site should be **sheltered** from winter winds.

### Tips

Winter hazel makes a welcome addition to woodland borders with light shade. It can also be grown as a specimen and should be planted within view of the house or in a frequently passed location, so you will be reminded to take a moment to enjoy the fragrant flowers.

### Recommended

*C. pauciflora* is a Long Island Gold Medal Award winner. It is a bushy, spreading shrub that bears short, narrow, dangling clusters of fragrant, pale yellow, primrose-like flowers in early spring. The bronzy young leaves mature to bright green.

*Cut a few winter hazel branches in January or February and put them in a vase indoors to force them into very early bloom. The fragrant flowers will foreshadow spring delights to come.*

**Also called:** buttercup winter hazel
**Features:** bushy, spreading, deciduous shrub; fragrant, yellow, spring flowers; attractive foliage **Height:** 4–6' **Spread:** 5–7'
**Hardiness:** zones 6–8

# Witchhazel
## *Hamamelis*

*H. x intermedia* 'Jelena' (above)
*H. x intermedia* (right)

Witchhazel is an investment in happiness. It blooms in mid- to late winter, the flowers last for weeks and their spicy fragrance awakens the senses. Then in fall, the handsome leaves develop overlapping bands of orange, yellow and red.

## Growing
Witchhazels grow best in a **sheltered** spot with **full sun** or **light shade**. The soil should be of **average fertility, neutral to acidic, moist** and **well drained**.

## Tips
Witchhazels work well individually or in groups. They can be used as specimen plants, in shrub or mixed borders or in woodland gardens. As small trees, they are ideal for space-limited gardens.

## Recommended
*H. x **intermedia*** is a vase-shaped, spreading shrub that bears fragrant clusters of yellow, orange or red flowers. The leaves turn attractive shades of orange, red and bronze in fall. Cultivars with flowers in shades of red, yellow or orange are available.

*The unique flowers have long, narrow, crinkled petals that give the plant a spidery appearance when in bloom. If the weather gets too cold, the petals will roll up, protecting the flowers and extending the flowering season.*

**Features:** spreading, deciduous shrub or small tree; fragrant, early-spring flowers; summer and fall foliage; habit **Height:** 6–20' **Spread:** 6–20' **Hardiness:** zones 5–9

# Yew

*Taxus*

*T. x media* 'Green Wave' (above), *T. x media* (below)

From sweeping hedges to commanding specimens, yews can serve many purposes in the garden.

### Growing

Yews grow well in any light conditions from **full sun to full shade**. The soil should be **fertile, moist** and **well drained**. These trees tolerate windy, dry and polluted conditions, as well as soils of any acidity. They dislike excessive heat, however, and on the hotter south or southwest side of a building they may suffer needle scorch.

### Tips

Yews can be used in borders or as specimens, hedges, topiaries and groundcovers.

### Recommended

*T. x media* (English Japanese yew), a cross between *T. baccata* (English yew) and *T. cuspidata* (Japanese yew), has the vigor of the English yew and the cold hardiness of the Japanese yew. It forms a rounded, upright tree or shrub, though the size and form can vary among the many cultivars.

*Male and female flowers are borne on separate plants. Both sexes must be present for the attractive red arils (seed cups) to form.*

**Features:** evergreen; conical or columnar tree, or bushy or spreading shrub; foliage; habit; red seed cups **Height:** 1–70'
**Spread:** 1–30' **Hardiness:** zones 4–7

# Blushing Knockout
## Modern Shrub Rose

This Long Island Gold Medal Award winner was introduced in 2004, and with its rounded habit and spring-through-fall blooming, it is quickly becoming a garden favorite.

### Growing
Blushing Knockout grows best in **full sun** but tolerates light afternoon shade. The soil should be **fertile, humus rich, slightly acidic, moist** and **well drained**. There is no need to deadhead because the blooms are self-cleaning. Flowers form on new wood, so trim plants back in early spring to encourage lots of new growth.

### Tips
This rose, with its long blooming period and tidy habit, deserves a place of prominence in your garden. Plant it near an entryway or as a focal point, or arrange several plants in a mixed or shrub border. This rose can even be planted to form a low, informal hedge.

### Recommended
*R.* **'Blushing Knockout'** ('Radyod') has a rounded and bushy form and mossy green, blue-tinged leaves. The profuse, light pink flowers turn pale pink to white as they mature.

*If you're concerned that roses need too much care, you'll appreciate the hardiness and disease resistance of this low-maintenance beauty. Diseases such as black spot and powdery mildew and pests like Japanese beetles don't pose a threat to this lovely rose.*

**Features:** rounded habit; light pink fading to pale pink or white, spring-to-fall flowers; disease resistance **Height:** 2–4'
**Spread:** 2–4' **Hardiness:** zones 4–9

# Electric Blanket

Groundcover · Carpet Rose

Electric Blanket's disease resistance makes it an easy rose to grow.

### Growing

Electric Blanket grows best in **full sun**. The soil should be **fertile, humus rich, slightly acidic, moist** and **well drained**, though this durable rose adapts to a variety of soil conditions. It is resistant to black spot and other rose diseases. Deadhead to encourage continuous blooming.

*Electric Blanket is a winner of the German Rose Society's equivalent to the All-America Rose Selections Award, which is the highest honor a rose can win in that country.*

### Tips

Electric Blanket is a versatile rose that works well in a variety of situations. Plant it in small groups in borders, cottage-style gardens and rose gardens. Another option is to mass plant it as a groundcover on slopes and banks where mowing is undesirable, and along driveways and walkways. It also makes an attractive low hedge.

### Recommended

*R.* **'Electric Blanket'** ('Korpancom') is a compact, mounding plant with glossy, dark green leaves. It bears clusters of salmon pink to coral pink flowers from late spring to the first hard frost of fall.

**Features:** compact, mounding habit; salmon pink to coral pink flowers; light sweet fragrant flowers from spring to fall  **Height:** 12–24" **Spread:** 18–30" **Hardiness:** zones 5–9

# Lady Elsie May

## Modern Shrub Rose

This floriferous, disease-resistant rose was a 2005 All-America Rose Selections winner.

### Growing
Lady Elsie May grows best in **full sun.** The soil should be **fertile, humus rich, slightly acidic, moist** and **well drained,** though these plants are durable and adaptable.

### Tips
Lady Elsie May makes an excellent choice for mass planting and is tall enough to provide a lovely screen for a patio. It can be grown in a container or as a specimen plant.

### Recommended
*R.* **'Lady Elsie May'** ('Angelsie') is a vigorous and uniform, upright, spreading plant with waxy, dark green foliage. Slightly fragrant, long-stemmed, coral pink flowers, suitable for cutting, open from darker pink buds.

*The compact size of Lady Elsie May makes it a suitable choice for a large planter, so this lovely rose can be enjoyed by people with balcony gardens as well as by those with ground-level gardens.*

**Features:** upright, spreading habit; semi-double, coral pink to pink, spring-through-fall flowers; disease resistance **Height:** 24–36" **Spread:** 24" **Hardiness:** zones 5–10

# Moondance

Floribunda Rose

This rose will be introduced in 2007 as both an All-America Rose Selections winner and as a Floribunda of the Year winner.

## Growing

Moondance grows best in **full sun**. The soil should be **fertile, humus rich, slightly acidic, moist** and **well drained**. Cut back dead or damaged growth in spring as the buds emerge.

## Tips

This gorgeous rose is extremely vigorous and tall, so it makes a lovely specimen that can be trained as a low climber. Plant it where you will be able to enjoy the fragrance of the flowers.

## Recommended

*R.* '**Moondance**' is a vigorous; upright rose with glossy, dark green foliage. It bears large clusters of creamy white, double flowers in flushes from late spring to fall.

*It is easy to create delightful floral arrangements with Moondance because of its exceptionally beautiful and fragrant blossoms and its long stems.*

**Features:** tall, vigorous habit; spicy raspberry-scented, creamy white, spring-to-fall blooms; disease resistance **Height:** 4–5'
**Spread:** 2–3' **Hardiness:** zones 5–9

# Peace

## Hybrid Tea Rose

One of the easiest roses to grow, Peace has been called the Rose of the Century.

### Growing

Peace grows best in **full sun** in a warm, **sheltered** location. Soil should be **fertile, humus rich, slightly acidic, moist** and **well drained**. Amend the soil with plenty of **organic matter** to improve its nutrient content, texture, water retention and drainage. Some New York gardeners will have to provide winter protection to overwinter this rose successfully.

### Tips

Peace is an ideal cut-flower variety. It is suitable for rose beds, hedges and borders and is an excellent choice for a standard. It responds well to moderate pruning but resents hard pruning.

### Recommended

*R.* **'Peace'** is an upright rose with glossy, dark green foliage. It bears fully double, yellow flowers tinged with pink from early summer to fall. The pink is more pronounced during hot weather. This rose is fairly disease resistant, though some problems with black spot can occur during wet seasons.

*In 1976 Peace was the first rose selected as the World's Favorite Rose by the World Federation of Rose Societies. It remains one of the most celebrated and popular roses in history.*

**Features:** vigorous grower; mild fruity-scented, spring-to-fall flowers; soft yellow flowers with delicate pink tinging **Height:** 5–6'
**Spread:** 3–4' **Hardiness:** zones 5–9

# Queen Elizabeth

Grandiflora Rose

The grandiflora classification was originally created to accommodate this rose. Queen Elizabeth is one of the most widely grown and best-loved roses. This magnificent rose can easily live more than six decades.

### Growing

Queen Elizabeth grows best in **full sun**. Soil should be **average to fertile, humus rich, slightly acidic, moist** and **well drained,** but this durable rose adapts to most soils and tolerates high heat and humidity. Prune plants back to 5–7 canes and to 5–7 buds each spring.

### Tips

Queen Elizabeth is a trouble-free rose that makes a good addition to mixed borders and beds. It can also be used to form a hedge, or grown as a specimen or in a large planter. The sturdy stems on which the flowers are borne are useful for floral arrangements. Queen Elizabeth is one of the loveliest roses and one of the easiest to grow.

### Recommended

*R.* **'Queen Elizabeth'** is a bushy plant with glossy, dark green foliage and dark stems. The robust, pink, cup-shaped, double flowers may be borne singly or in clusters of several flowers.

*This incredible and long-lasting rose, named after Queen Elizabeth II of England, was a 1955 All-America Rose Selections winner and in 1979 was named the World's Favorite Rose.*

**Features:** glossy, dark green, disease-resistant foliage; lightly scented, soft pearly pink, summer-to-fall flowers **Height:** 4–6' **Spread:** 30–36" **Hardiness:** zones 5–8

# Rainbow Knockout

## Modern Shrub Rose

This beauty will be introduced in 2007 as an All-America Rose Selections winner and will make an outstanding addition to the Knockout Series of roses. Rainbow Knockout is a compact, disease-resistant, shrub-like rose that produces blooms continually throughout the growing season.

## Growing

Rainbow Knockout grows best in **full sun** but tolerates light afternoon shade. The soil should be **fertile, humus rich, slightly acidic, moist** and **well drained**.

## Tips

This dense grower and prolific bloomer makes a fabulous hedge. It can also be used in beds and borders and as a focal point in a smaller garden.

**Features:** rounded habit; spring-through-fall flowers; orange to pink flowers with creamy or yellow centers; disease resistance
**Height:** 2–3'  **Spread:** 2–3'
**Hardiness:** zones 4–9

## Recommended

*R.* **'Rainbow Knockout'** ('Radcor') forms a dense, bushy mound. It has glossy, dark green leaves and bears orange to pink flowers with yellow or creamy centers from spring to the first hard frost of fall. Bright orange hips follow in fall.

*All the roses in the Knockout Series share the traits of excellent blooming and disease resistance. Other roses in the series include Knockout, Double Knockout and Pink Knockout.*

# Red Ribbons
Groundcover · Carpet Rose

Red Ribbons has been recognized around the world for its hardiness, charm and versatility.

## Growing
Red Ribbons grows best in **full sun**. The soil should be **fertile, humus rich, slightly acidic, moist** and **well drained,** but this rose is fairly adaptable to a variety of soil conditions.

*Its bright red petals and yellow stamens make Red Ribbons stand out in the garden*

## Tips
Naturally vigorous, dense, low and spreading, this rose looks wonderful cascading down embankments, growing up short pillars or planted in groups. It also works well in difficult locations.

## Recommended
*R.* **'Red Ribbons'** is vigorous, dense and low growing, with dark green foliage. It bears clusters of bright red flowers from early summer to fall.

**Features:** low, spreading habit; summer to fall, semi-double to double, lightly fragrant, bright deep red flowers; disease resistance
**Height:** 2' **Spread:** 4–5'
**Hardiness:** zones 4–9

# Black-Eyed Susan Vine
*Thunbergia*

*P*ut smiles in your garden with the black-eyed Susan vine. This lovely plant will certainly brighten up the garden.

### Growing
Black-eyed Susan vines do well in **full sun, partial shade** or **light shade**. Grow them in **fertile, moist, well-drained soil** that is **high in organic matter**.

### Tips
Black-eyed Susan vines can be trained to twine up and around fences, walls, trees and shrubs as well as trellises. They are also attractive trailing down from the top of a rock garden or rock wall or growing in mixed containers and hanging baskets.

### Recommended
*T. alata* is a vigorous, twining climber. It bears yellow flowers, often with dark centers, in summer and fall. Cultivars with large flowers in yellow, orange or white are available.

*T. grandiflora* (blue trumpet vine) is a twining climber that bears stunning, pale violet-blue flowers. **'Alba'** has white flowers.

*T. alata* (above & below)

*The blooms are actually trumpet-shaped, with the dark centers forming a tube.*

**Features:** twining habit; yellow, orange, violet-blue, creamy white, dark-centered flowers
**Height:** 5' or more **Spread:** 5' or more
**Hardiness:** tender perennial treated as an annual

# Clematis

*Clematis*

*Josephim x long bluming 49.99* (handwritten)

C. 'Etoile Violette' (above), C. x *jackmanii* (below)

There are so many species, hybrids and cultivars of clematis that it is possible to have one in bloom all season long.

## Growing

Clematis plants prefer **full sun** but tolerate partial shade. The soil should be **fertile, humus rich, moist** and **well drained**. These vines enjoy warm, sunny weather, but the roots prefer to be cool. A thick layer of mulch or a planting of low, shade-providing perennials will protect the tender roots. Clematis are quite cold hardy but will fare best when protected from winter wind. The rootball of vining clematis should be planted about 2" beneath the surface of the soil.

## Tips

Clematis vines can climb up structures such as trellises, railings, fences and arbors. They can also be allowed to grow over shrubs and up trees and can be used as groundcover.

## Recommended

There are many species, hybrids and cultivars of clematis, with varying flower forms, blooming times and sizes. Check with your local garden center to see what is available.

*Plumbago 14.99* (handwritten)
*Bissett 13.99* (handwritten)

**Features:** twining habit; blue, purple, pink, yellow, red, white, early- to late-summer flowers; decorative seedheads **Height:** 10–17' or more **Spread:** 5' or more **Hardiness:** zones 3–8

# Climbing Hydrangea
## *Hydrangea*

*H. anomala* subsp. *petiolaris* (above & below)

A mature climbing hydrangea can cover an entire wall. With its dark, glossy leaves and delicate, lacy flowers, it is quite possibly one of the most stunning climbing plants available.

### Growing

Hydrangeas prefer **partial or light shade,** but they tolerate both full sun and full shade. The soil should be of **average to high fertility, humus rich, moist** and **well drained**. These plants perform best in cool, moist conditions, so be sure to mulch their roots.

### Tips

Climbing hydrangea climbs up trees, walls, fences, pergolas and arbors. It clings to walls by means of aerial roots, so it needs no support, just a somewhat textured surface. It also grows over rocks, can be used as a groundcover and can be trained to form a small tree or shrub. It can be slow to start, but once established it will take off, covering the area that it is growing against.

### Recommended

***H. anomala* subsp. *petiolaris*** (*H. petiolaris*) is a Long Island Gold Medal Award winner. It is a clinging vine with dark, glossy green leaves that sometimes turn an attractive yellow in fall. For more than a month in mid-summer, the vine is covered with white, lacy-looking flowers, and the entire plant appears to be veiled in a lacy mist.

*Climbing hydrangea will produce the most flowers when it is exposed to some direct sunlight each day.*

**Features:** flowers; clinging habit; exfoliating bark **Height:** 50–80' **Spread:** 50–80'
**Hardiness:** zones 4–8

# Honeysuckle
### *Lonicera*

L. *sempervirens* (above)
L. x *brownii* 'Dropmore Scarlet' (below)

Honeysuckles can be rampant twining vines, but with careful consideration and placement they won't overrun your garden. The wonderfully sweet fragrance of the flowers makes any effort worthwhile.

### Growing
Honeysuckles grow well in **full sun** or **partial shade**. The soil should be **average to fertile, humus rich, moist** and **well drained**.

### Tips
Honeysuckle can be trained to grow up a trellis, fence, arbor or other structure. In a large container near a porch, it will ramble over the edges of the pot and up the railings with reckless abandon.

### Recommended
There are dozens of honeysuckle species, hybrids and cultivars. Check with your local garden center to see what is available. The following are two popular species.

**L. caprifolium** (Italian honeysuckle, Italian woodbine) bears fragrant, creamy white or yellow flowers in late spring and early summer.

**L. sempervirens** (trumpet honeysuckle, coral honeysuckle) bears orange or red flowers in late spring and early summer. Many cultivars and hybrids are available with flowers in yellow, red or scarlet. **L. x brownii 'Dropmore Scarlet,'** one of the hardiest of the climbing honeysuckles, is cold hardy to Zone 4. It bears bright red flowers for most of the summer.

**Features:** late-spring and early-summer flowers; twining habit; fruit **Height:** 6–20' **Spread:** 6–20' **Hardiness:** zones 5–8

# Hops
*Humulus*

*I*f you sit near hops for an afternoon, you might actually be
able to watch the plant grow. Two
feet of growth in a single day is not
uncommon in early summer.

### Growing
Hops grow best in **full sun**. The
soil should be **average to fertile,
humus rich, moist** and **well
drained,** but established plants
adapt to most conditions if they
are well watered for the first few
years.

### Tips
Hops quickly twine around any
sturdy support to create a screen
or shade a patio or deck. Provide
a pergola, arbor, porch rail or even
a telephone pole for hops to grow
up. Most trellises are too delicate
for this vigorous grower.

### Recommended
*H. lupulus* is a fast-growing, twining vine with rough-textured,
bright green stems and leaves. The
fragrant, pale green, cone-like fruit
ripen to beige. They are produced only
on the female plants and are used to flavor and preserve beer. A cultivar with
golden yellow foliage is also available.

H. lupulus (above & below)

*As true perennials, hops send up new
shoots from the ground each year. The
previous year's growth needs to be cleared
away each fall or spring.*

**Features:** twining habit; dense growth; cone-
like, pale green, late-summer fruit that ripen
to beige **Height:** 10–20' or more
**Spread:** 10–20' or more
**Hardiness:** zones 3–8

# Japanese Hydrangea Vine
*Schizophragma*

*his vine is similar in appearance to climbing hydrangea, but it has a few interesting cultivars to add variety.

### Growing
Japanese hydrangea vine grows well in **full sun** or **partial shade**. The soil should be **average to fertile, humus rich, moist** and **well drained**.

This vine will have trouble clinging to a smooth-surfaced wall. Attach a few supports to the wall and tie the vines to these. The dense growth will eventually hide the support.

### Tips
This vine will cling to any rough surface and looks attractive climbing a wall, fence, tree, pergola or arbor. It can also be used as a groundcover on a bank or it can be allowed to grow up or over a rock wall.

*S. hydrangeoides* (above & below)

### Recommended
***S. hydrangeoides*** is an attractive climbing vine similar in appearance to climbing hydrangea. It bears lacy clusters of white flowers in mid-summer. **'Moonlight'** has silvery blue foliage. **'Roseum'** bears clusters of pink flowers.

*This elegant vine adds a touch of glamour to even the most ordinary-looking home.*

**Features:** clinging habit; dark green or silvery foliage; white or pink flowers **Height:** up to 40'
**Spread:** up to 40' **Hardiness:** zones 5–8

# Mandevilla

*Mandevilla*

This lovely twining vine will add a touch of the tropics and lots of color to your garden.

## Growing

Mandevilla grows best in **full sun** but enjoys some protection from the heat of the midday sun. The soil should be **average to fertile, moist** and **well drained**.

## Tips

Treat these tender woody vines as annuals and add them to mixed containers and hanging baskets. They can grow 4–6' in a single summer. Provide a sturdy support for them to grow up, and cut them back a bit at the end of the season. Bring them indoors before the first frost. Keep them in a sunny but cool room and ensure that the soil stays evenly moist but not soggy until the next spring, when you can move them back outdoors for the summer. Overwintering mandevilla vine in a greenhouse is ideal.

## Recommended

Several species and cultivars of mandevilla are available. Most are woody twining vines that bear pink flowers in summer. Check with your local garden center in spring to see what is available.

*Wash your hands thoroughly after handling this plant because the sap can cause skin irritation or, if ingested, stomach upset.*

**Features:** twining vine; attractive foliage and flowers **Height:** 5–10' **Spread:** 5–10' **Hardiness:** tender woody vine; grown as an annual

M. splendens 'Rosacea' (above), M. boiviensis (below)

# Morning Glory

*Ipomoea*

*I. tricolor* (above & below)

I. alba, *commonly called "moonflower," is a twining climber that bears sweet-scented, white flowers that open only at night. It is similar in size and habit to the two morning glories listed here.*

M orning glory's brightly colored flowers are produced in abundance, and this vine gives even the dullest fence or wall a splash of excitement.

## Growing

Morning glory grows best in **full sun**. The soil should be of **average fertility, light** and **well drained,** though this plant adapts to most soil conditions. Morning glory twines around narrow objects to climb and must be provided with a trellis or wires if it is grown against a fence with broad boards, a wall or other surface it won't be able to wind around.

## Tips

Morning glory vines can be grown on fences, walls, trees, trellises and arbors. As groundcovers, morning glories will grow over any objects they encounter. They can also be grown in hanging baskets or containers where they will spill over the edges.

## Recommended

*I. purpurea* is a twining climber that bears trumpet-shaped flowers in shades of purple, blue, pink or white. Cultivars are available.

*I. tricolor* is a twining climber that bears trumpet-shaped flowers in shades of blue and purple, often with lighter or white centers. Many cultivars are available, including **'Heavenly Blue'** with white-centered, sky blue flowers.

**Features:** fast-growing, twining habit; flowers; foliage **Height:** 6–12' **Spread:** 6–12' **Hardiness:** tender annual

# Sweet Pea
## *Lathyrus*

Sweet peas are among the most enchanting annuals. Their fragrance is intoxicating, and the flowers, in double tones and shimmering shades, look like no other annual in the garden.

### Growing
Sweet peas prefer **full sun** but tolerate light shade. The soil should be **fertile, high in organic matter, moist** and **well drained**. The plants tolerate light frost.

Soak seeds in water for 24 hours or nick them with a nail file before planting them. Planting a second crop of sweet peas about a month after the first one will ensure a longer blooming period. Deadhead all spent blooms.

### Tips
Sweet peas will grow up or over poles, trellises, fences and rocks. They cling by wrapping tendrils around whatever they are growing up, so they do best when they have a rough surface, chain-link fence, small twigs or a net to cling to.

### Recommended
There are many cultivars of **L. odoratus** available, though many are now small, bushy and compact rather than climbing.

*L. odoratus* cultivars (above & below)

*Newer sweet pea cultivars often have less fragrant flowers than old-fashioned cultivars. Look for heritage varieties to enjoy the most fragrant flowers.*

**Features:** clinging habit; pink, red, purple, lavender, blue, salmon, pale yellow, peach, white, bicolored, summer flowers **Height:** 1–6' **Spread:** 6–12" **Hardiness:** hardy annual

# Virginia Creeper • Boston Ivy
## *Parthenocissus*

P. quinquefolia (above & below)

*Virginia creeper and Boston ivy can cover the sides of buildings and help to keep the buildings cool in the summer heat. Cut the plants back as needed to keep windows and doors accessible.*

Virginia creeper and Boston ivy are handsome vines that establish quickly and provide an air of age and permanence, even on new structures.

### Growing
These vines grow well in any light from **full sun to full shade**. The soil should be **fertile** and **well drained**. The plants will adapt to clay or sandy soils.

### Tips
Virginia creepers can cover an entire building, given enough time. They do not require support because they have clinging rootlets that can adhere to just about any surface, even smooth wood, vinyl or metal. Give the plants lots of space and let them cover a wall, fence or arbor. Take care, however, that this vine doesn't overpower other desirable plants.

### Recommended
The following two species are very similar, except for the shape of the leaves.

*P. quinquefolia* (Virginia creeper, woodbine) has dark green foliage. Each leaf, divided into five leaflets, turns flame red in fall. (Zones 3–9)

*P. tricuspidata* (Boston ivy, Japanese creeper) has dark green, three-lobed leaves that turn red in fall. This species is not quite as hardy as Virginia creeper. (Zones 4–8)

**Features:** summer and fall foliage; clinging habit **Height:** 30–70' **Spread:** 30–70' **Hardiness:** zones 3–9

# Wisteria

*Wisteria*

*L*oose clusters of purple flowers hang like lace from the branches of the classic wisteria. A gardener willing to use garden shears can create beautiful tree forms and attractive arbor specimens.

## Growing

Wisterias grow well in **full sun** or **partial shade**. The soil should be of **average fertility, moist** and **well drained**. Vines grown in too fertile of a soil produce lots of vegetative growth but very few flowers. Don't plant wisteria near a lawn where fertilizer may leach over to your vine.

## Tips

These vines require something to twine around, such as an arbor or other sturdy structure. You can also train a wisteria to form a small tree. Try to select a permanent site; wisterias don't like to be moved. These vigorous vines may send up suckers and can root wherever branches touch the ground.

## Recommended

*W. floribunda* (Japanese wisteria) bears long, pendulous clusters of fragrant, blue, purple, pink or white flowers in late spring before the leaves emerge. Long, bean-like pods follow.

*W. sinensis* (Chinese wisteria) bears long, pendant clusters of fragrant, blue-purple flowers in late spring. **'Alba'** bears white flowers.

*W. sinensis* (above & below)

*All parts of wisterias, including the seeds in the long, bean-like pods, are poisonous.*

---

**Features:** late-spring flowers; foliage; twining habit **Height:** 20–50' or more
**Spread:** 20–50' or more
**Hardiness:** zones 4–9

# Canna Lily
## *Canna*

Canna lilies are stunning, dramatic plants that give height as well as an exotic flair to the garden.

### Growing
Canna lilies grow best in **full sun** in a **sheltered** location. The soil should be **fertile, moist** and **well drained**. Plant the bulb under 1" of soil in spring, once the soil has warmed. You can start the plants earlier in containers indoors to get a head start on the growing season. Deadhead to prolong blooming.

### Tips
Canna lilies can be grown in beds or borders. They make dramatic specimen plants and can even be included in large planters.

### Recommended
A wide range of canna lilies are available, including cultivars and hybrids with green, bronzy, purple or yellow and green striped foliage. Flowers may be white, red, orange, pink, yellow or bicolored. Dwarf cultivars that grow 18–28" tall are also available.

*C.* 'Red King Humbert' (above & below)

*The rhizomes can be lifted after the foliage dies back in fall. Clean off any clinging soil and store them in a cool, frost-free location in peat moss. Check on them regularly through the winter and if they are starting to sprout, pot them and move them to a bright window until they can be moved outdoors.*

**Features:** decorative foliage; summer flowers
**Height:** 18"–6'  **Spread:** 20–36"
**Hardiness:** zones 7–9; grown as an annual

# Crocus

*Crocus*

*C.* x *vernus* cultivar (above & below)

rocuses are a sure sign that spring is just around the corner. They are sometimes seen blooming up through a late-winter snowfall.

## Growing

Crocuses grow well in **full sun** or **light, dappled shade**. The soil should be of **poor to average fertility, gritty** and **well drained**. The corms are planted about 4" deep in fall.

## Tips

Crocuses are almost always planted in groups. You can plant drifts of them in your lawn to provide interest and color while the grass is still dormant and doesn't need mowing. By the time the lawn starts growing, the crocuses will have finished blooming. In beds and borders crocuses can be left to naturalize. Groups of plants will fill in and spread out to provide a bright welcome in spring.

## Recommended

Many crocus species, hybrids and cultivars are available. The spring-flowering crocus most people are familiar with is ***C.* x *vernus*** (Dutch crocus). Many cultivars are available with flowers in shades of purple, yellow and white, sometimes bicolored or with darker veins.

*Saffron is obtained from the dried, crushed stigmas of C. sativus. Six plants produce enough spice for one recipe. This fall-blooming plant is hardy to zone 6 and can be grown successfully in the mildest parts of New York.*

**Features:** early-spring flowers **Height:** 2–6"
**Spread:** 2–4" **Hardiness:** zones 3–8

# Cyclamen

*Cyclamen*

*C. hederifolium* (above & below)

This miniature plant makes a lovely addition to a shade garden. The attractively patterned foliage and fall flowers in shades of pink or white provide a contrast of colors in a season dominated by foliage and flowers of yellows and oranges.

## Growing

Cyclamen grows best in **light or partial shade**. The soil should be **fertile, humus rich** and **well drained**. Add a layer of

*These plants take a while to establish and spread, but the charming, down-facing flowers and marbled foliage of these beauties are worth waiting for.*

compost to the soil each spring. Plant the bulb under 1" of soil.

## Tips

Cyclamens are attractive plants to use in shaded beds, borders, rock gardens and woodland gardens. If planted in containers, they may need winter protection because of the greater root temperature fluctuations.

## Recommended

*C. hederifolium* forms a low clump of triangular to heart-shaped, evergreen foliage from fall to mid-summer. The dark green foliage is patterned with light green and silvery markings. Pink or white flowers are produced in fall. Plants usually go dormant during the heat of summer.

**Also called:** hardy cyclamen
**Features:** attractive evergreen foliage; pink or white fall flowers **Height:** 4–6"
**Spread:** 6–8" **Hardiness:** zones 5–9

# Daffodil

## *Narcissus*

*M*any gardeners automatically think of large, yellow, trumpet-shaped flowers when they think of daffodils, but there is plenty of variation in color, form and size among these delightful plants.

### Growing

Daffodils grow best in **full sun** or **light, dappled shade**. The soil should be **average to fertile, moist** and **well drained**. Bulbs should be planted in fall, 2–8" deep, depending on the size of the bulb. The bigger the bulb, the deeper it should be planted. A rule of thumb is to measure the bulb from top to bottom and multiply that number by three to know how deeply to plant it.

### Tips

Daffodils are often planted where they can be left to naturalize, such as in the light shade beneath a tree or in a woodland garden. In mixed beds and borders, the faded leaves are hidden by the summer foliage of other plants.

### Recommended

Many species, hybrids and cultivars of daffodils are available. Flowers come in shades of white, yellow, peach, orange and pink, and some are also bicolored. Flowers range from 1½–6" across, and they can be solitary or borne in clusters. There are about 12 flower form categories of daffodils.

*The cup in the center of a daffodil is called the corona, and the group of petals that surrounds the corona is called the perianth.*

**Also called:** narcissus **Features:** spring flowers **Height:** 4–24" **Spread:** 4–12" **Hardiness:** zones 3–9

# Dahlia

*Dahlia*

Mixed cultivars in a cutting bed (above)

**D**ahlia flowers have an astonishing variation in size, shape and color. Surely at least one of these magnificent flowers appeals to almost everyone.

*Dahlia breeders have yet to develop true blue, scented or frost-hardy selections.*

## Growing

Dahlias prefer **full sun**. The soil should be **fertile, rich in organic matter, moist** and **well drained**. All dahlias are tender tuberous perennials treated as annuals. Start the tubers early indoors by planting them 1" deep under the soil. The tubers can be lifted in fall after the first frost and stored over winter in peat moss. Deadhead to keep plants tidy and blooming.

## Tips

Dahlias make attractive, colorful additions to a mixed border. The smaller varieties make good edging plants and the larger ones are good alternatives to shrubs. Varieties with unusual or interesting flowers make attractive specimen plants. Taller varieties with large flowers may need staking.

## Recommended

Most of the many dahlia hybrids are purchased as and grown from tubers, but a few can be started from seed. Many hybrids are sold based on flower shape, such as collarette, decorative or peony-flowered. The flowers range in size from 2–12" and are available in shades of purple, pink, white, yellow, orange and red with some of them bicolored. Check with your local garden center, mail order catalogue or online for availability.

**Features:** summer flowers; attractive foliage; bushy habit **Height:** 8"–5' **Spread:** 8–18" **Hardiness:** tender perennial grown as an annual

# Flowering Onion

*Allium*

Tall flowering onions with striking, ball-like flowers are sure to attract attention in the garden.

## Growing

Flowering onions grow best in **full sun**. The soil should be **fertile, moist** and **well drained**. Plant the bulbs in fall, 2–4" deep, depending on the size of the bulb.

## Tips

Flowering onions are best planted in groups in a bed or border where they can be left to self-seed and naturalize. The foliage, which tends to fade just as the plants come into flower, can be hidden with groundcover or a low, bushy companion plant.

*A. giganteum* (above), *A. cernuum* (below)

## Recommended

Several flowering onion species, hybrids and cultivars have gained popularity for their decorative pink, purple, white, yellow, blue or maroon flowers. **A. aflatunense** has dense, globe-like clusters of lavender flowers. **A. caeruleum** (blue globe onion) features globe-like clusters of blue flowers. **A. cernuum** (nodding or wild onion) sports loose, drooping clusters of pink flowers. **A. giganteum** (giant onion) is a big plant up to 6' tall, with large, globe-shaped clusters of pinkish purple flowers.

*Though the leaves have an onion scent when bruised, the flowers are often sweetly fragrant.*

**Features:** summer flowers; cylindrical or strap-shaped leaves **Height:** 1–6' **Spread:** 2–12" **Hardiness:** zones 3–9

# Gladiolus

*Gladiolus*

*G.* x *hortulanus* Grandiflorus (above), *G.* 'Homecoming' (below)

Perhaps best known as a cut flower, gladiolus adds an air of extravagance to the garden

## Growing

Gladiolus grows best in **full sun** and tolerates partial shade. The soil should be **fertile, humus rich, moist** and **well drained**. Flower spikes may need staking and a sheltered location out of the wind to prevent the flower spikes from blowing over.

Plant corms in spring, 4–6" deep, once the soil has warmed. Corms can also be started early indoors. Plant a few corms each week for about a month to prolong the blooming period.

## Tips

Planted in groups in beds and borders, gladiolus makes a bold statement. Corms can be pulled up in fall and stored in damp peat moss in a cool, frost-free location for winter.

## Recommended

*G.* x *hortulanus* is a huge group of hybrids. Gladiolus flowers come in almost every imaginable shade, except blue. Plants are commonly grouped into three classifications. **Grandiflorus** are the best known, with each corm producing a single spike of large, often ruffled flowers. **Nanus,** the hardiest group, can survive in zone 3 with winter protection and produces several spikes of up to seven flowers. **Primulinus** produces a single spike of up to 23 flowers that are more spaced out on the spike than those of grandiflorus.

**Features:** brightly colored, mid- to late-summer flowers **Height:** 18"–6' **Spread:** 6–12"
**Hardiness:** zones 8–10; grown as an annual

# Glory-in-the-Snow

*Chionodoxa*

*C. luciliae* (above), *C. forbesii* (below)

Perfect companions for crocuses, glory-in-the-snow flowers brighten the spring garden as winter begins to fade.

## Growing

Glory-in-the-snow grows best in **full sun**. Soil should be of **average fertility** and **well drained**. A wet winter soil should be avoided because these plants can quickly develop root rot or bulb rot. Plant the bulbs 3" deep in fall.

## Tips

Because they appreciate dry winter soil, these bulbs are a good choice for plantings under the overhang of the house. They also make lovely additions to rock and alpine gardens. These plants self-seed and can be left to naturalize.

## Recommended

*C. forbesii* forms a clump of narrow leaves. It bears clusters of 4–12 blue, star-shaped flowers with white centers in early spring. It grows 4–8" tall and spreads 2–4".

*C. luciliae* forms a clump of narrow leaves and bears clusters of two or three blue, star-shaped flowers in early spring. It grows up to 6" tall and spreads 2–4".

**Also called:** glory-of-the-snow
**Features:** star-shaped, blue, early-spring flowers **Height:** 4–8" **Spread:** 2–4"
**Hardiness:** zones 3–8

# Grape Hyacinth
*Muscari*

M. botryoides (above), M. armeniacum (below)

It's not difficult to see where these bulbs get their common name. The purple or blue flowers, borne densely clustered on spikes, do indeed look like bunches of grapes.

## Growing

Grape hyacinths grow best in **full sun** but will tolerate partial shade and light shade. The soil should be **average to fertile, humus rich, moist** and **well drained**. Plant bulbs 3–4" deep in fall.

*Propagate these plants by dividing the small plants (offsets) that grow in around the parent plant.*

## Tips

Planted in masses or small groups, grape hyacinth makes a great spring accent plant, blending well with other bulbs and spring-blooming plants. It can also be left to naturalize in borders

## Recommended

*M. armeniacum* (Armenian grape hyacinth) forms a low-growing clump of narrow, grass-like leaves. The bright blue or purple flowers are densely clustered on spikes. (Zones 4–8)

*M. botryoides* (common grape hyacinth) is similar in appearance to Armenian grape hyacinth, but the plants are much smaller. Flowers are pale blue. '**Album**' has white flowers. (Zones 2–8)

*M. comosum* '**Plumosum**' has feathery, bright red-violet flowers. The flower spikes are plumey rather than grape-like. (Zones 4–8)

Features: blue, white, yellow, purple, spring flowers; good for naturalizing Height: 4–8" Spread: 6–12" Hardiness: zones 2–8

# Hyacinth

*Hyacinthus*

The fragrance of these flowers, though it can be overpowering indoors, is delightful outdoors.

## Growing

Hyacinth grows best in **full sun** but tolerates partial shade. The soil should be of **average fertility, moist** and **well drained**. Plant bulbs 4–8" deep in fall. The colder your winters are, the deeper you should plant these bulbs.

## Tips

Plant hyacinths in groups of three to seven amongst the other plants in your beds and borders for a bold splash of color and an unforgettable fragrance in your spring garden. The fading foliage of the small groups will be hidden as the other plants in the beds fill in for the summer.

## Recommended

*H. orientalis* is a perennial bulb that forms a clump of strap-shaped leaves. A spike of fragrant, star-shaped flowers is produced in spring. The species bears light purple flowers, but many cultivars have been developed with flowers in a huge range of colors, including shades of purple, pink, red, yellow, orange, blue and white.

*H. orientalis* cultivar (above & below)

*Despite their delicate appearance, hyacinths are actually native to the rocky terrain and high altitudes of the mountains of Turkey, Syria and Lebanon.*

**Features:** spring flowers in shades of purple, blue, pink, red, yellow, orange, white
**Height:** 8–12" **Spread:** 3–6"
**Hardiness:** zones 5–9; often treated as an annual

# Lily
## *Lilium*

L. Asiatic hybrids (above), L. 'Stargazer' (below)

*Lily bulbs should be planted in fall before the first frost, but they can also be planted in spring if bulbs are available.*

Decorative clusters of large, richly colored blooms grace these tall plants. Flowers are produced at different times of the season, depending on the hybrid, and it is possible to have lilies blooming all season long if a variety of cultivars are chosen.

### Growing
Lilies grow best in **full sun,** but they like to have their roots shaded. The soil should be **rich in organic matter, fertile, moist** and **well drained**. The bulb should be planted 4–6" deep.

### Tips
Lilies are often grouped in beds and borders and can be naturalized in woodland gardens and near water features. These plants are narrow but tall; plant at least three plants together to create some volume.

### Recommended
The many species, hybrids and cultivars available are grouped by type. Visit your local garden center, check bulb catalogues or go online to see what is available. The following are two popular groups of lilies. **Asiatic hybrids** bear clusters of flowers in early summer or mid-summer and are available in a wide range of colors. **Oriental hybrids** bear clusters of large, fragrant flowers in mid- and late summer. Flower colors are usually white, pink or red.

**Features:** early-, mid- or late-season flowers, in shades of orange, yellow, peach, pink, purple, red, white **Height:** 2–5' **Spread:** 12" **Hardiness:** zones 4–8

# Snowdrops
## *Galanthus*

Snowdrops are the first bulbs to bloom, sometimes as early as late winter. Their delicate, white, nodding flowers pierce through the snow, giving us a taste of spring.

### Growing

Snowdrops prefer to grow in **partial or light shade** but tolerate all light conditions from full sun to full shade. The soil should be of **average fertility, humus rich, moist** and **well drained**. These plants prefer it if the soil doesn't dry out completely in summer. Plant bulbs 4" deep and 2" apart. Divide or move plants as soon as possible after flowering is complete in spring.

### Tips

Snowdrops are popular bulbs for naturalizing. They can be planted into mixed beds and borders, thriving at the feet of deciduous shrubs and in meadow plantings.

### Recommended

*G. elwesii* (giant snowdrops) forms a clump of bright green, strap-shaped leaves and grows 5–12" tall. It bears fragrant, white flowers in late winter.

*G. nivalis* (common snowdrops) forms a clump of long, narrow leaves. It bears small, white, fragrant flowers in winter and grows about 4" tall. **'Flore Pleno'** bears double flowers.

*These lovely plants are adaptable and hardy.*

G. elwesii (above), G. nivalis (below)

**Features:** white, early-spring flowers
**Height:** 4–12" **Spread:** 2–6"
**Hardiness:** zones 3–9

# Spanish Bluebell

*Hyacinthoides*

*H. hispanica* cultivar (above), *H. hispanica* (below)

Spanish bluebells are a real gem for naturalizing because, unlike many bulbs, they form really good clumping masses as they mature. Also, they can last for decades.

### Growing

Spanish bluebells grow best in **light, dappled shade**. The soil should be of **average fertility, humus rich, moist** and **well drained,** though these bulbs are quite tolerant of a variety of soils. Plant bulbs about 3" deep in fall.

### Tips

These bulbs are ideal for naturalizing in just about any lightly shaded situation. Include them in woodland gardens and under shrubs in beds and borders.

### Recommended

*H. hispanica* forms a clump of strap-shaped leaves and produces spikes of blue, bell-shaped flowers. It grows about 16" tall and spreads about 12". Cultivars with purple, white or pinkish purple flowers are also available.

*Native to Spain, Portugal and northern Africa, Spanish bluebells have been successfully grown in many parts of the world.*

Also called: bluebell Features: blue, purple, white, pink, spring flowers; clump-forming habit; suitable for naturalizing
Height: 12–18" Spread: 8–16"
Hardiness: zones 4–9

# Tulip

*Tulipa*

Tulips, with their beautiful, often garishly colored flowers, are a welcome sight as we enjoy the warm days of spring.

## Growing

Tulips grow best in **full sun**. The flowers tend to bend toward the stronger light when these plants are grown in light or partial shade. The soil should be **fertile** and **well drained**. Plant bulbs in fall, 4–6" deep, depending on the size of the bulb. Bulbs that have been cold treated can be planted in spring. Though tulips can repeat bloom, many hybrids perform best if planted new each year. Species and older cultivars are the best choice for naturalizing.

## Tips

Tulips provide the best display when mass planted or planted in groups in flowerbeds and borders. They can also be grown in containers and can be forced to bloom early in pots indoors. Some of the species and older cultivars can be naturalized in meadow and wildflower gardens.

## Recommended

There are about 100 species of tulips and thousands of hybrids and cultivars. Tulips are generally divided into 15 groups based on bloom time and flower appearance. They come in dozens of shades, with many bicolored or multi-colored varieties. Check with your local garden center, bulb catalogue or online in early fall for the best selection.

**Features:** spring flowers **Height:** 6–30"
**Spread:** 2–8" **Hardiness:** zones 3–8;
often treated as annuals

*T.* hybrids (above & below)

*During the tulipomania of the 1630s, the bulbs were worth many times their weight in gold, and many tulip speculators lost massive fortunes when the mania ended.*

# Basil
*Ocimum*

The sweet, fragrant leaves of fresh basil add a delicious spicy flavor to salads and tomato-based dishes and sauces.

### Growing
Basil grows best in a warm, **sheltered** location in **full sun**. The soil should be **fertile, moist** and **well drained**. Pinch tips regularly to encourage bushy growth. Plant out or direct sow seed after frost danger has passed in spring.

### Tips
Though basil will grow best in a warm spot outdoors in the garden, it can be grown successfully indoors in a pot by a bright window to provide you with fresh leaves all year long.

### Recommended
*O. basilicum* is one of the most popular culinary herbs. There are dozens of varieties including ones with large or tiny, green or purple and smooth or ruffled leaves.

*O. basilicum* 'Genovese' and 'Cinnamon' (above)
*O. basilicum* 'Genovese' (below)

*O. x citriodorum* (lemon basil) is a deliciously lemon-scented and -flavored basil for soups, salads, fish and potatoes, as well as tomato dishes.

*Basil is a good companion plant for tomatoes—both like warm, moist growing conditions, and when you pick tomatoes for a salad you'll also remember to include a few sprigs or leaves of basil.*

**Features:** fragrant, decorative leaves
**Height:** 12–24" **Spread:** 12–18"
**Hardiness:** tender annual

# Chives
*Allium*

The delicate onion flavor of chives is best enjoyed fresh. Mix chives into dips or sprinkle them on salads and baked potatoes.

## Growing

Chives grow best in **full sun**. The soil should be **fertile, moist** and **well drained,** but chives adapt to most soil conditions. These plants are easy to start from seed, but they do like the soil temperature to stay above 65° F before they germinate, so seeds started directly in the garden are unlikely to sprout before early summer.

## Tips

Chives are decorative enough to be included in a mixed or herbaceous border and can be left to naturalize. In an herb garden, chives should be given plenty of space to allow self-seeding.

## Recommended

**A. schoenoprasum** forms a clump of bright green, cylindrical leaves. Clusters of pinkish purple flowers are produced in early and mid-summer. Varieties with white or pink flowers are available.

*A. schoenoprasum* (above & below)

*Chives will spread with reckless abandon as the clumps grow larger and the plants self-seed.*

**Features:** foliage; form; flowers
**Height:** 8–24"  **Spread:** 12" or more
**Hardiness:** zones 3–9

# Dill

*Anethum*

*A. graveolens* (above & below)

Dill leaves and seeds are probably best known for their use as pickling herbs, though they have a wide variety of other culinary uses.

## Growing

Dill grows best in **full sun** in a **sheltered** location out of strong winds. The soil should be of **poor to average fertility, moist** and **well drained**. Sow the seeds every couple of weeks in spring and early summer to ensure a regular supply of leaves. Plants should not be grown near fennel because they will cross-pollinate and the seeds of both plants will lose their distinct flavors.

## Tips

With its feathery leaves, dill is an attractive addition to a mixed bed or border. It can be included in a vegetable garden, but it does well in any sunny location. It also attracts beneficial predatory insects to the garden.

## Recommended

*A. graveolens* forms a clump of feathery foliage. Clusters of yellow flowers are borne at the tops of sturdy stems.

*A popular Scandinavian dish called gravalax is made by marinating a fillet of salmon with the leaves and seeds of dill.*

**Features:** feathery, edible foliage; yellow, summer flowers; edible seeds **Height:** 2–5'
**Spread:** 12" or more **Hardiness:** annual

# Mint

*Mentha*

The cool, refreshing flavor of mint lends itself to tea and other hot or cold beverages. Mint sauce, made from freshly chopped leaves, is often served with lamb.

### Growing

Mint grows well in **full sun** or **partial shade**. The soil should be **average to fertile, humus rich** and **moist**. Mint spreads vigorously by rhizomes and may need a barrier in the soil to restrict its spread.

### Tips

Mint is a great groundcover for damp spots. It grows well along ditches that may be wet only periodically. It also can be used in beds and borders but may overwhelm less vigorous plants.

The flowers attract bees, butterflies and other pollinators to the garden.

### Recommended

There are many species, hybrids and cultivars of mint. **Spearmint** (*M. spicata*), **peppermint** (*M.* x *piperita*) and **orange mint** (*M.* x *piperita citrata*) are three of the most commonly grown culinary varieties. There are also more decorative varieties with variegated or curly leaves as well as varieties with unusual, fruit-scented leaves.

*M.* x *piperita* 'Chocolate' (above)
*M.* x *piperita citrata* (below)

*A few sprigs of fresh mint added to a pitcher of iced tea gives it an added zip.*

**Features:** fragrant foliage; purple, pink, white, summer flowers **Height:** 6–36" **Spread:** 36" or more **Hardiness:** zones 4–8

# Oregano • Marjoram
*Origanum*

Oregano and marjoram are two of the best-known and most frequently used herbs. They are popular in stuffings, soups and stews, and no pizza is complete until it has been sprinkled with fresh or dried oregano leaves.

## Growing

Oregano and marjoram grow best in **full sun**. The soil should be of **poor to average fertility, neutral to alkaline** and **well drained**. The flowers attract pollinators to the garden.

## Tips

These bushy perennials make lovely additions to any border, and you can trim them to form low hedges.

## Recommended

*O. majorana* (marjoram) is upright and shrubby with light green, hairy leaves. It bears white or pink flowers in summer and can be grown as an annual where it is not hardy.

*O. vulgare* **var. hirtum** (oregano, Greek oregano) is the most flavorful culinary variety of oregano. The low, bushy plant has hairy, gray-green leaves and bears white flowers. Many other interesting varieties of *O. vulgare* are available, including those with golden, variegated or curly leaves.

*O. vulgare* 'Aureum' (above & below)

*In Greek* oros *means "mountain" and* ganos *means "joy" or "beauty," so oregano translates as "joy (or beauty) of the mountain."*

**Features:** fragrant foliage; white or pink, summer flowers; bushy habit **Height:** 12–32"
**Spread:** 8–18" **Hardiness:** zones 5–9

# Parsley

*Petroselinum*

*T*hough usually used as a garnish, parsley is rich in vitamins and minerals and is reputed to freshen the breath after garlic- or onion-rich foods are eaten.

## Growing

Parsley grows well in **full sun** or **partial shade**. The soil should be of **average to rich fertility, humus rich, moist** and **well drained**. Directly sow seeds in the garden because the plants resent transplanting. If you start seeds early, use peat pots so the plants can be potted or planted into the soil without disruption.

## Tips

Parsley should be started where you want it to grow, because it doesn't transplant well. Containers of parsley can be kept close to the kitchen door for easy picking. The bright green leaves and compact growth habit make parsley a good edging plant for beds and borders.

## Recommended

*P. crispum* forms a clump of bright green, divided leaves. This plant is biennial but is usually grown as an annual because it is the leaves that are desired and not flowers or seeds. Cultivars may have flat or curly leaves. Flat leaves are more flavorful and curly are more decorative. Dwarf cultivars are also available.

*P. crispum* (above), *P. crispum* var. *crispum* (below)

*Parsley leaves make a tasty and nutritious addition to salads. Tear freshly picked leaves and sprinkle them over or mix them into your mixed greens.*

**Features:** attractive foliage **Height:** 8–24"
**Spread:** 12–24" **Hardiness:** zones 5–8; grown as an annual

# Rosemary
*Rosmarinus*

The needle-like leaves of rosemary are used to flavor a wide variety of culinary dishes, including chicken, pork, lamb, rice, tomato and egg dishes.

## Growing
Rosemary prefers **full sun** but tolerates partial shade. The soil should be of **poor to average fertility** and **well drained**. These tender shrubs must be moved indoors for the winter.

## Tips
In New York, where rosemary is not hardy, it is usually grown in a container as a specimen or with other plants. Low-growing, spreading plants can be included in a rock garden or along the top of a retaining wall or can be grown in hanging baskets.

## Recommended
*R. officinalis* is a dense, bushy, evergreen shrub with narrow, dark green leaves. The habit varies somewhat between cultivars from strongly upright to prostrate and spreading. Flowers are usually in shades of blue, but pink-flowered cultivars are available. Cultivars that can survive in zone 6 in a sheltered location with winter protection are available. Plants rarely reach their mature size when grown in containers.

*R. officinalis* (above & below)

*To overwinter a container-grown plant, keep it in very light or partial shade outdoors in summer, then put it in a sunny window, under a skylight or in a greenhouse for the winter. Keep it well watered, but allow it to dry out slightly between waterings.*

**Features:** fragrant, evergreen foliage; bright blue, sometimes pink, summer flowers
**Height:** 8"–4'  **Spread:** 1–4'
**Hardiness:** zones 8–10

# Sage

*Salvia*

Sage is perhaps best known as a flavoring for stuffing, but it has a great range of uses in soups, stews, sausages, dumplings and the like.

### Growing

Sage prefers **full sun** but tolerates light shade. The soil should be of **average fertility** and **well drained**. These plants benefit from a light mulch of compost each year. They are drought tolerant once established.

### Tips

Sage will add volume to the middle of a border. It is also useful as an edging or feature plant near the front of the border. Alternately, sage can be grown in mixed planters.

### Recommended

*S. officinalis* is a woody, mounding plant with soft, gray-green leaves. Spikes of light purple flowers appear in early and midsummer. Many cultivars with attractive foliage are available, including the silver-leaved **'Berggarten,'** the purple-leaved **'Purpurea,'** the yellow-margined **'Icterina,'** and the purple-green-and-cream-variegated **'Tricolor,'** which has a pink flush to the new growth.

S. officinalis 'Icterina' (above)
S. officinalis 'Purpurea' (below)

*The ancient Greeks used sage as a medicinal and culinary herb, and it continues to be used for both of those purposes today.*

**Features:** fragrant, decorative foliage; blue or purple, summer flowers  **Height:** 12–24"
**Spread:** 18–36"  **Hardiness:** zones 5–8

# Thyme
*Thymus*

T. vulgaris (above), T. x citriodorus (below)

*These plants are bee magnets when blooming; thyme honey is pleasantly herbal and goes very well with biscuits.*

Thyme is a popular culinary herb used in soups, stews, casseroles and with roasts.

## Growing
Thyme prefers **full sun**. The soil should be **neutral to alkaline** and of **poor to average fertility**. **Good drainage** is essential. It is beneficial to work leaf mold and sharp limestone gravel into the soil to improve structure and drainage.

## Tips
Thyme is useful for sunny, dry locations at the front of borders, between or beside paving stones, on rock gardens and rock walls, and in containers.

Once the plants have finished flowering, shear them back by about half to encourage new growth and prevent the plants from becoming too woody.

## Recommended
*T. x citriodorus* (lemon-scented thyme) forms a mound of dark green, lemon-scented foliage. The flowers are pale pink. Cultivars with silver- or gold-margined leaves are available.

*T. vulgaris* (common thyme) forms a bushy mound of dark green leaves. The flowers may be purple, pink or white. Cultivars with variegated leaves are available.

**Features:** bushy habit; fragrant, decorative foliage; purple, pink or white flowers
**Height:** 8–16" **Spread:** 8–16"
**Hardiness:** zones 4–9

# Ajuga
*Ajuga*

*A. reptans* 'Caitlin's Giant' (above & below)

hy have grass when you can cover the ground with these lovely ramblers? Often described as rampant runners, ajugas grow best where they can roam freely.

## Growing
Ajugas develop the best leaf color in **partial shade** or **light shade** but tolerate full shade; excessive sun may scorch the leaves. Any **well-drained soil** is suitable. Divide these vigorous plants any time during the growing season.

## Tips
Ajugas make excellent groundcovers for difficult sites such as exposed slopes and dense shade. They are also attractive in shrub borders, where their dense growth prevents the spread of all but the most tenacious weeds.

## Recommended
*A. genevensis* (Geneva bugleweed, blue bugleweed) is an upright, noninvasive species that bears blue, white or pink, spring flowers.

*A. pyramidalis* 'Metallica Crispa' (upright bugleweed) is a very slow-growing plant with bronzy, crinkly foliage and violet-blue flowers.

*A. reptans* is a low, quick-spreading groundcover. The many cultivars are grown for their colorful, often variegated foliage.

**Also called:** bugleweed **Features:** purple, pink, bronze, green, white or variegated foliage; purple, blue, pink, white, late-spring to early-summer flowers **Height:** 3–12" **Spread:** 6–36" **Hardiness:** zones 3–8

# Artemisia
*Artemisia*

A. *ludoviciana* 'Silver Queen' (above)
A. *ludoviciana* 'Valerie Finnis' (below)

$\mathcal{M}$ost of the artemisias are valued for their silvery foliage, not their flowers. Silver is the ultimate blending color in the garden, because it enhances every other hue it is combined with.

## Growing
Artemisias grow best in **full sun**. The soil should be of **low to average fertility** and **well drained**. These plants dislike wet, humid conditions.

When artemisias begin to look straggly, cut them back hard to encourage new growth and maintain a neater form. Divide them every year or two, when plant clumps appear to be thinning in the centers.

## Tips
Use artemisias in rock gardens and borders. Their silvery gray foliage makes them good backdrop plants to use behind brightly colored flowers, and they are also useful for filling in spaces between other plants. Smaller forms may be used to create knot gardens. Some artemisias can spread and become invasive in the garden.

## Recommended
*A. ludoviciana* (white sage, silver sage, western mugwort) is an upright, clump-forming plant with silvery white foliage. The species is not grown as often as its cultivars. (Zones 4–8)

*A.* x **'Powis Castle'** is a compact, mounding, shrubby plant with feathery, silvery gray foliage. This hybrid is reliably hardy to zone 6, but it can also grow in colder regions if planted with winter protection in a sheltered site.

*A. schmidtiana* (silvermound artemisia) is a low, dense, mound-forming perennial with feathery, hairy, silvery gray foliage. **'Nana'** (dwarf silvermound) is very compact and grows only half the size of the species. (Zones 4–8)

---

**Also called:** wormwood, sage
**Features:** silvery gray, feathery or deeply lobed foliage **Height:** 6"–6' **Spread:** 12–36"
**Hardiness:** zones 3–8

# Caladium
*Caladium*

If you are looking for a plant that has delicate and interesting foliage and will tolerate shade, then the caladium is for you.

## Growing
Caladium grows well in **partial, light** or **full shade**. The soil should be of **average fertility, humus rich, slightly acidic, moist** and **well drained**. This plant has tuberous roots and can be lifted in fall once the leaves die back. Over the winter, it can be stored in slightly moist peat moss in a cool, frost free location.

## Tips
Caladiums make great additions to mixed containers, adding welcome color to shaded patios, porches and balconies. They can also be grown in mixed beds and borders.

## Recommended
*C. bicolor* (heart of Jesus) is a tuberous perennial with large leaves marked with dark green and red, white or pink. Many cultivars are available with unique variations in leaf variegation.

*These plants have been popular as houseplants for years. They have only recently been added to the repertoire of annual plant selections.*

C. bicolor cultivar (above)
C. bicolor 'Sweetheart' (below)

---

**Also called:** angel wings, elephant's ears
**Features:** dark green foliage, marked, spotted or splashed with red, pink or white
**Height:** 24" **Spread:** 24" **Hardiness:** tender perennial; grown as an annual

# Coleus
*Solenostemon (Coleus)*

S. *scutellarioides* mixed cultivars (above & below)

There is a coleus for everyone. From brash yellows, oranges and reds to deep maroon and rose selections, the colors, textures and variations are almost limitless.

*Coleus can be trained to grow into a standard (tree) form by pinching off the side branches as they grow. Once the plant reaches the desired height, pinch from the top to create a bushy rounded plant atop the stem.*

## Growing

Coleus prefers to grow in **light or partial shade,** but tolerates full shade if the shade isn't too dense and full sun if the plants are watered regularly. The soil should be of **rich to average fertility, humus rich, moist** and **well drained**.

Place the seeds in a refrigerator for one or two days before planting them (the cold temperature there will assist in breaking the seeds' dormancy). The seeds need light to germinate, so just leave them on the soil surface. Seedlings will be green at first, and then leaf variegation develops as the plants mature.

## Tips

The bold, colorful foliage makes coleus dramatic when the plants are grouped together as edging plants or in beds, borders or mixed containers. Coleus can also be grown indoors as a houseplant in a bright room.

When flower buds develop, it is best to pinch them off, because the plants tend to stretch out and become less attractive after they flower.

## Recommended

*S. scutellarioides (Coleus blumei* var. *verschaffeltii)* forms a bushy mound of foliage. The leaf edges range from slightly toothed to very ruffled. The leaves are usually multi-colored, with shades ranging from pale greenish yellow to deep purple-black. Dozens of cultivars are available but many cannot be started from seed.

**Features:** brightly colored foliage; light purple flowers **Height:** 6–36" **Spread:** usually equal to height **Hardiness:** tender perennial; grown as an annual

# Dusty Miller

*Senecio*

S. cineraria 'Cirrus' (above), S. cineraria (below)

Dusty miller makes an artful addition to planters, window boxes and mixed borders where the soft, silvery gray, deeply lobed foliage makes a good backdrop to show off the brightly colored flowers of other annuals.

## Growing

Dusty miller prefers **full sun** but tolerates light shade. The soil should be of **average fertility** and **well drained**.

## Tips

The soft, silvery, lacy leaves of this plant are its main feature. Dusty miller is used primarily as an edging plant, but is also useful in beds, borders and containers.

Pinch off the flowers before they bloom. They aren't showy and they steal energy that would otherwise go to producing more foliage.

## Recommended

**S. cineraria** forms a mound of fuzzy, silvery gray, lobed or finely divided foliage. Many cultivars have been developed with impressive foliage colors and shapes.

*Mix dusty miller with geraniums, begonias or cockscombs to bring out the vibrant colors of those flowers.*

**Features:** silvery foliage; neat habit
**Height:** 12–24" **Spread:** equal to height or slightly narrower **Hardiness:** tender perennial grown as an annual

# Fescue

*Festuca*

F. glauca 'Elijah Blue' (above)
F. glauca (below)

This finely leaved ornamental grass forms tufted clumps that resemble pin cushions. Its metallic blue coloring adds an all-season cooling accent to the garden.

## Growing

Fescue thrives in **full sun** to **light shade**. The soil should be of **average fertility**, **moist** and **well drained**. These plants are drought tolerant once established. Fescue emerges early in spring, so shear it back to 1" above the crown in late winter or early spring, before the new growth emerges. Shear off flower stalks just above the foliage to keep plants tidy and to prevent self-seeding.

## Tips

With its fine texture and distinct blue color, this grass can be used as a single specimen in a rock garden or a container planting. Plant fescue in drifts to create a sea of blue or a handsome edge to a bed, border or pathway. It looks attractive in both formal and informal gardens.

## Recommended

*F. glauca* forms tidy, tufted clumps of fine, blue-toned foliage and loose clusters of flowers in May and June. Cultivars and hybrids come in varying heights and in shades ranging from blue to olive green. **'Elijah Blue'** is a popular selection.

*If you like the look of blue grass, you might also like the large, coarse-textured blue oat grass,* Helicotrichon sempervirens, *which can grow 4' tall when in flower.*

**Also called:** blue fescue **Features:** blue to blue-green foliage; color persists into winter; habit **Height:** 6–12" **Spread:** 10–12" **Hardiness:** zones 4–8

# Fountain Grass

*Pennisetum*

The low maintenance requirements and graceful form of fountain grass make it easy to incorporate in your garden. This plant will soften any landscape, even in winter.

### Growing

Fountain grass likes **full sun.** The soil should be of **average fertility** and **well drained**. Plants are drought tolerant once established. Fountain grass may self-seed, but not in a troublesome way.

Shear perennials back in early spring, and divide them when they start to die out in the center.

### Tips

Fountain grasses can be used as individual specimen plants, in group plantings and drifts, or they can be combined with flowering annuals, perennials, shrubs and other ornamental grasses. Annual selections are often planted in mixed containers or beds to add height and stature.

### Recommended

Both perennial and annual fountain grasses are available.

Popular perennials include ***P. alopecuroides*** '**Hameln**' (dwarf perennial fountain grass), a compact cultivar with silvery white plumes and narrow, dark green foliage that turns gold in fall, and

*P. orientale* 'Karley Rose' (above)

***P. orientale*** (Oriental fountain grass), with tall, blue-green foliage and large, silvery white flowers (zones 6–9, with winter protection).

---

**Features:** arching, fountain-like habit; green, blue-green, silvery, burgundy or purplish black foliage; silvery white or pinkish purple flowers; winter interest **Height:** 2–5' **Spread:** 24–36" **Hardiness:** zones 5–9; some are grown as annuals

*The name* Pennisetum alopecuroides *refers to the plume-like flower spikes that resemble a fox's tail. In Latin,* penna *means "feather," and* seta *means "bristle";* alopekos *is the Greek word for "fox."*

# Heuchera

*Heuchera*

*H. x brizoides 'Firefly' (above), H. sanguineum (below)*

*Heucheras have a strange habit of pushing themselves up out of the soil because of their shallow root systems. Mulch in fall if the plants begin heaving from the ground.*

From soft yellow-greens and oranges to midnight purples and silvery, dappled maroons, heucheras offer a great variety of foliage options for a perennial garden.

## Growing

Heucheras grow best in **light or partial shade**; full sun can bleach out the foliage colors, and the plants become leggy in full shade. The soil should be of **average fertility, humus rich, neutral to alkaline, moist** and **well drained**. Good air circulation is essential. Deadhead to prolong the blooming period.

Every two or three years, dig up your heucheras and remove the oldest, woodiest roots and stems. Divide the plants at this time, if desired, then replant them with the crown at or just above soil level.

## Tips

Use heucheras as edging plants or in clusters. They are lovely in woodland gardens and as groundcovers for low-traffic areas. Combine different foliage types for an interesting display.

## Recommended

There are dozens of beautiful heuchera species, hybrids and cultivars with almost limitless variations of foliage markings and colors. Visit your local garden center or check out a mail-order catalog or on-line to see what is available.

**Also called:** coral bells, alum root
**Features:** very decorative foliage; red, pink, white, yellow, purple, spring or summer flowers
**Height:** 1–4'  **Spread:** 6–24"
**Hardiness:** zones 3–9

# Lungwort
*Pulmonaria*

*P. saccharata* cultivar (above & below)

The wide array of lungworts have highly attractive foliage that ranges in color from apple green to silver-spotted and from olive to dark emerald.

## Growing

Lungworts prefer **partial to full shade**. The soil should be **fertile, humus rich, moist** and **well drained**. Rot can occur in very wet soil.

Divide in early summer after flowering or in fall. Provide the newly planted divisions with lots of water to help them re-establish.

## Tips

Lungworts make useful and attractive groundcovers for shady borders, woodland gardens and pond and stream edges.

## Recommended

*P. longifolia* (long-leaved lungwort) forms a dense clump of long, narrow, white-spotted green leaves and bears clusters of blue flowers.

*P. officinalis* (common lungwort, spotted dog) forms a loose clump of evergreen foliage, spotted with white. The flowers open pink and mature to blue. Cultivars are available.

*P. saccharata* (Bethlehem sage) forms a compact clump of large, white-spotted, evergreen leaves and purple, red or white flowers. Many cultivars are available.

**Features:** decorative mottled foliage; blue, red, pink, white, spring flowers
**Height:** 8–24" **Spread:** 8–36"
**Hardiness:** zones 3–8

# Maidenhair Fern

*Adiantum*

A. *pedatum* (above & below)

These charming and delicate-looking native ferns add a graceful touch to any woodland planting. Their unique habit and texture will stand out in your garden.

## Growing

Maidenhair fern grows well in **light or partial shade** and tolerates full shade. The soil should be of **average fertility, humus rich, slightly acidic** and **moist**. This plant rarely needs dividing, but if you want more of these lovely ferns you can divide it in spring.

## Tips

Maidenhair ferns will do well in any shaded spot in the garden. Include them in rock gardens, woodland gardens, shaded borders and beneath shade trees. They also make an attractive addition to a shaded planting next to a water feature or on a slope where the foliage can be seen when it sways in the breeze.

## Recommended

**A. pedatum** forms a spreading mound of delicate, arching fronds. Light green leaflets stand out against the black stems, and the whole plant turns bright yellow in fall. Spores are produced on the undersides of the leaflets.

*Try growing the fine-textured and delicate maidenhair fern with hostas, pulmonarias and brunneras and enjoy the lovely contrast in texture.*

**Also called:** northern maidenhair
**Features:** deciduous, perennial fern; summer and fall foliage; habit **Height:** 12–24"
**Spread:** 12–24" **Hardiness:** zones 2–8

# Ostrich Fern
## *Matteuccia*

This popular classic fern is revered for its delicious emerging spring fronds and its stately, vase-shaped habit.

### Growing
Ostrich fern prefers **partial or light shade** but tolerates full shade and even full sun if the soil is kept moist. The soil should be **average to fertile, humus rich, neutral to acidic** and **moist**. Leaves may scorch if the soil is not moist enough. These ferns are aggressive spreaders that reproduce by spores. Unwanted plants can be pulled up and composted or given away.

### Tips
These ferns appreciate a moist woodland garden and are often found growing wild alongside woodland streams and creeks. Useful in shaded borders, ostrich ferns are quick to spread, to the delight of people who enjoy the young fronds as a culinary delicacy.

*M. struthiopteris* (above & below)

### Recommended
***M. struthiopteris*** (*M. pennsylvanica*) forms a circular cluster of slightly arching, feathery fronds. Stiff, brown, fertile fronds, covered in reproductive spores, stick up in the center of the cluster in late summer and persist through winter. They are popular choices for dried arrangements.

*Ostrich ferns are also grown commercially for their edible fiddleheads. The tightly coiled, new spring fronds taste delicious lightly steamed and served with butter. Remove the bitter, reddish brown, papery coating before steaming.*

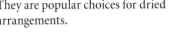

**Also called:** fiddlehead fern
**Features:** perennial fern; foliage; habit
**Height:** 3–5' **Spread:** 12–36" or more
**Hardiness:** zones 3–8

# Pachysandra
*Pachysandra*

*P. terminalis* (above & below)

The low-maintenance pachysandra is one of the most popular groundcovers. Its rhizomatous roots colonize quickly to form a dense blanket over the ground.

## Growing

Pachysandra prefers **light to full shade** and tolerates partial shade. Any soil that is **moist, acidic, humus rich** and **well drained** is good. Plants can be propagated easily from cuttings or by division.

*Interplant this popular groundcover with spring bulbs, hostas or ferns, or use it as an underplanting for deciduous trees and shrubs with contrasting foliage colors.*

## Tips

Pachysandras are durable groundcovers for under trees, in shady borders and in woodland gardens. The foliage is considered evergreen, but winter-scorched shoots may need to be removed in spring. Shear or mow old plantings in early spring to rejuvenate them.

## Recommended

*P. terminalis* (Japanese spurge) forms a low mass of foliage rosettes. It grows about 8" tall and can spread almost indefinitely. **'Variegata'** has white margins or mottled silver foliage, but it is not as vigorous as the species. **'Green Sheen'** has, as its name implies, exceptionally glossy leaves that are smaller than those of the species.

---

**Also called:** Japanese spurge
**Features:** perennial evergreen groundcover; habit; inconspicuous, fragrant, white, spring flowers **Height:** 8" **Spread:** 12–18" or more
**Hardiness:** zones 3–8

# Sweet Potato Vine
## *Ipomoea*

*I. batatas* 'Margarita' (above & below)

This vigorous, rambling annual plant with lime green, bruised purple or green, pink-and-cream-variegated leaves can make any gardener look like a genius.

## Growing
Grow sweet potato vine in **full sun**. Any type of soil will do, but a **light, well-drained soil** of **poor to average fertility** is preferred.

## Tips
Sweet potato vine is a great addition to mixed planters, window boxes and hanging baskets. In a rock garden it will scramble about, and along the top of a retaining wall it will cascade over the edge. Though this plant is a vine, its bushy habit and colorful leaves make it a useful foliage plant.

## Recommended
*I. batatas* (sweet potato vine) is a twining climber that is grown for its attractive foliage rather than its flowers. Several cultivars are available.

*Unlike the more aggressive morning glory species, sweet potato vine drapes politely over the sides of containers or spreads neatly over the soil beneath taller plants.*

**Features:** decorative foliage
**Height:** about 12" **Spread:** up to 10'
**Hardiness:** grown as an annual

# Sweet Woodruff

*Galium*

G. *odoratum* (above & below)

Sweet woodruff is a groundcover with abundant good qualities: attractive, light green foliage that smells like newly mown hay; profuse, white, spring flowers; and the ability to fill in garden spaces without taking over.

## Growing

This plant prefers **partial shade**. It will grow well, but will not bloom well, in

*Sweet woodruff's vanilla-scented dried leaves and flowers were once used to scent bed linens and are often added to potpourri.*

full shade. The soil should be **humus rich, slightly acidic** and **evenly moist**. Sweet woodruff competes well with other plant roots and does well where some other groundcovers such as vinca fail to thrive.

## Tips

Sweet woodruff makes a fast-spreading woodland groundcover. It forms a beautiful, green carpet and thrives in the same conditions as azaleas and rhododendrons. Interplant it with spring bulbs for a fantastic display in spring.

## Recommended

**G. *odoratum*** is a low, spreading groundcover. It bears clusters of star-shaped, white flowers in a flush in late spring, and these blooms continue to appear sporadically through mid-summer.

---

**Features:** deciduous perennial groundcover; white, late-spring to mid-summer flowers; fragrant foliage; habit **Height:** 12–18"
**Spread:** indefinite **Hardiness:** zones 3–8

# Glossary

**Acidic soil:** soil with a pH lower than 7.0

**Annual:** a plant that germinates, flowers, sets seed and dies in one growing season

**Alkaline soil:** soil with a pH higher than 7.0

**Basal foliage:** leaves that form from the crown, at the base of the plant

**Bract:** a modified leaf at the base of a flower or flower cluster

**Corm:** a bulb-like, food-storing, underground stem, resembling a bulb without scales

**Crown:** the part of the plant at or just below soil level where the shoots join the roots

**Cultivar:** a cultivated plant variety with one or more distinct differences from the species, e.g., in flower color or disease resistance

**Deadhead:** to remove spent flowers to maintain a neat appearance and encourage a longer blooming season

**Direct sow:** to sow seeds directly in the garden

**Dormancy:** a period of plant inactivity, usually during winter or unfavorable conditions

**Double flower:** a flower with an unusually large number of petals

**Espalier:** a tree trained from a young age to grow on a single plane—often along a wall or fence

**Genus:** a category of biological classification between the species and family levels; the first word in a scientific name indicates the genus

**Grafting:** a type of propagation in which a stem or bud of one plant is joined onto the rootstock of another plant of a closely related species

**Hardy:** capable of surviving unfavorable conditions, such as frost, without protection

**Hip:** the fruit of a rose, containing the seeds

**Humus:** decomposed or decomposing organic material in the soil

**Hybrid:** a plant resulting from natural or human-induced cross-breeding between varieties, species or genera

**Neutral soil:** soil with a pH of 7.0

**Offset:** a horizontal branch that forms at the base of a plant and produces new plants from buds at its tips

**Panicle:** a compound flower structure with groups of flowers on short stalks

**Perennial:** a plant that takes three or more years to complete its life cycle

**pH:** a measure of acidity or alkalinity; the soil pH influences availability of nutrients for plants

**Rhizome:** a root-like, food-storing stem that grows horizontally at or just below soil level, from which new shoots may emerge

**Rootball:** the root mass and surrounding soil of a plant

**Seedhead:** dried, inedible fruit that contains seeds; the fruiting stage of the inflorescence

**Self-seeding:** reproducing by means of seeds without human assistance, so that new plants constantly replace those that die

**Semi-double flower:** a flower with petals in two or three rings

**Single flower:** a flower with a single ring of typically four or five petals

**Species:** the fundamental unit of biological classification; the entity from which cultivars and varieties are derived

**Standard:** a shrub or small tree grown with an erect main stem, accomplished either through pruning and training or by grafting the plant onto a tall, straight stock

**Sucker:** a shoot that comes up from the root, often some distance from the plant; it can be separated to form a new plant once it develops its own roots

**Tender:** incapable of surviving the climatic conditions of a given region and requiring protection from frost or cold

**Tuber:** the thick section of a rhizome bearing nodes and buds

**Variegation:** foliage that has more than one color, often patched or striped or bearing leaf margins of a different color

**Variety:** a naturally occurring variant of a species

# Index of Recommended Species Plant Names

Entries in **bold** type indicate the main plant species; *italics* indicate botanical names.

# Author Biographies

**Maria Cinque** is a lawn and garden expert and is president of Cinque Associates Limited, a horticultural and environmental communications company. The Long Island–based gardening guru shares her expertise with millions of people through television appearances, radio interviews and print and web communications (www.mariacinque.com). Maria was one of the first female Agricultural Extension Agents/Specialists in the United States. She has an Associate Degree from Farmingdale State University of New York and Bachelor and Masters degrees in Plant Pathology and Horticulture from the University of Georgia. She has won numerous awards for her work in television, radio and print.

**Alison Beck** has gardened since she was a child. She has a diploma in Horticulture and a Bachelor of Arts in Creative Writing. Alison has co-authored many best-selling gardening guides. Her books showcase her talent for practical advice and her passion for gardening.

# Acknowledgments

My grandfather inspired me with his fascination and dedication to the everyday miracles of gardening. Motivated by his instincts and intuition, he shared his horticultural practices with me. My mother, motivated by her love of gardening, encouraged me to fulfill my passion for the beautiful and colorful world of horticulture. —*Maria Cinque*

Thanks to everyone who was involved in the creation of this book. I appreciate their time and effort. —*Alison Beck*